Literacy as Social Practice

Literacy as Social Practice

Primary Voices K–6

Edited by

Vivian Vasquez
American University

Kathryn A. Egawa
National Council of Teachers of English

Jerome C. Harste
Indiana University, Bloomington

Richard D. Thompson
Columbia Falls District 6, Montana

WITHDRAWN

National Council of Teachers of English
1111 W. Kenyon Road, Urbana, Illinois 61801-1096

Manuscript Editor: Lee Erwin
Staff Editor: Bonny Graham
Interior Design: Doug Burnett
Cover Design: Jenny Jensen Greenleaf

NCTE Stock Number: 29676

It is the policy of NCTE in its journals and other publications to provide a forum for the open discussion of ideas concerning the content and the teaching of English and the language arts. Publicity accorded to any particular point of view does not imply endorsement by the Executive Committee, the Board of Directors, or the membership at large, except in announcements of policy, where such endorsement is clearly specified.

Library of Congress Cataloging-in-Publication Data

Literacy as social practice : Primary voices K-6 / edited by Vivian Vasquez . . . [et al.].
     p. cm.
  Includes bibliographical references.
  ISBN 0-8141-2967-6 (pbk.)
  1. Language arts (Elementary)—Social aspects—United States. 2. Literacy—Social aspects—United States. 3. Critical pedagogy—United States. I. Vasquez, Vivian Maria. II. National Council of Teachers of English. III. Primary voices K-6.
  LB1576.L5526 2004
  372.6—dc22

                            2004013867

We would like to acknowledge the editors of **Primary Voices K–6** *and the communities of authors who over the years shared their teaching practices and teaching lives with us. It is to them that we dedicate this book.*

V. V., K. A. E., J. C. H., R. D. T.

Contents

IV. **Practices That Support Transformation**

Preface

"It is a journal designed primarily for teachers by teachers . . ."
Karen Smith

Primary Voices K–6, a unique journal because of its conception as a text written by different teams of elementary school educators, was published from 1993 to 2002. Karen Smith, one of the founders of the journal and former associate executive director of NCTE in charge of elementary and middle levels, began meeting and talking with members of NCTE's Elementary Section Steering Committee about how to better support elementary classroom teachers. Although they came up with many fresh, creative ideas, practical solutions were still lacking. Smith invited Diane Stephens, a university professor, to join her in brainstorming ways to realize the Steering Committee's charge. Their imaginations soared as they considered the many ways a national organization could support teachers.

Smith's and Stephens's imaginations didn't just soar; they took shape and became a reality, and for nine years the journal was a vehicle for groups of teachers interested in similar topics to share their insights and teaching practices. The author teams were a combination of experienced writers and those writing for publication for the first time. Each volume provided a close-up look at learning through rich descriptions of classrooms and samples of students' work. The journal was also known for suggesting helpful resources and strategies for literacy teaching, providing study groups such as those within the NCTE Reading Initiative network a valuable set of articles to use when taking up the study of a particular topic such as miscue analysis or inquiry-based learning. *Primary Voices K–6* has also been used as a text in teacher-education courses. Since the journal's first publication in 1993, other similarly useful resources have been developed, including the NCTE Elementary Section Steering Committee publication *School Talk* (www.ncte.org/pubs/journals/st) and the Reading Initiative Inquiry Studies. The official journal of the elementary section, *Language Arts,* has also evolved to include more teacher voices and practical resources. In light of the new resources available through NCTE, it was decided that *Primary Voices* had contributed as much as it uniquely could to the profession and so the final issue was published in October 2002. In this book our intent was to build on some of the theory and teaching practice found in past issues of *Primary Voices* and in doing so offer a new framework within which to read some of the articles.

We extend our deepest thanks to the editors of *Primary Voices* and to the communities of authors who shared their teaching practices and teaching lives with us.

Introduction

Reconceptua-lizing Literacy and Literacy Teaching

Over the years our definitions of literacy have changed. Although historical accounts and outlines chronicling these changes have appeared in print (Myers, 1996; Smith & Lambert Stock, 2003; Rosenblatt, 2003; Squire, 2003), there is no end to the process of change and so we continue to learn and add to this history. As we understand more about language and literacy, our conception of literacy changes and with it, ideally, our instructional practices. For example, we used to think about literacy as a commodity: a set of useful skills that you either had or didn't have and for which different teaching pedagogies and materials were developed, bought, and sold. During the mid-1990s, for instance, "[T]he differences among factions in the reading field resulted in fragmentation, disarray and division" (Dole & Osborn, 2003). The field was polarized along a number of dimensions; for example, phonics versus whole language, explicit versus implicit instruction, skills versus strategies, textbooks versus trade books, predictable versus decodable books, and reading groups versus literature circles (Graves, 1998).

More recently we have begun to think of literacy as sets of social practices. Social practices are particular ways of doing and being as well as particular ways of acting and talking that are rooted in life experiences. Since different people have different life experiences it follows that social practices are differentially available to various individuals and groups of people. This differential availability means that not everyone has equitable or equal access to literacy.

Conceptualizing literacy as social practices further implies that different cultures value and have access to different literacies or malleable sets of cultural practices, that is, a community's ways of being and doing. Luke and Freebody (1999) note that often these practices are shaped and reshaped by competing and contending social institutions such as school, church, and government. This is why for years teaching and learning literacy has been a topic of debate. These debates have resulted in such actions as the contestation of curricula by educators as well as the manufacture of literacy crises by governments.

Recently another "reshaping" of literacy instruction has hit the airwaves in what media and the current government refer to as "scientifically based balanced literacy" programs. The result can be seen in "district after district where the call for balance is too often read as a mandate to drop whatever you have been doing and add a half hour of systematic phonics to the already packed reading and writing program" (Egawa & Harste, 2001). According to Luke and Freebody, determining how to teach literacy cannot be simply "scientific," but rather has to involve moral, political, and cultural decisions about the kind of literate practices needed to enhance both peoples' agency over their own life trajectories or pathways and communities' intellectual, cultural, and semiotic or meaning-making resources in multimediated economies. *Multimediated* refers to the multiple modes of economic exchange now available around the globe, including the vast use of technology and media. This means that literacy instruction should ultimately be about the kind of literate citizenry and the kind of literate being that can and should be constructed to participate in our complex world.

For different teachers this means being able to set up different classroom environments that support a variety of literate practices. This point is exactly what the sections in this volume are about. They are demonstrations of ways in which some classroom teachers and educators have "practiced" and imagined teaching literacy. These recollections from the classroom were gathered from the corpus of *Primary Voices* journal articles published from 1993 to 2002.

It is important to note, however, that our ongoing reconceptualization of what makes up literacy and literacy teaching pushes us to realize that the practices we see reported here represent only the beginning of what is possible. As such we have included throughout the book discussions of what the future might look like: that is, how particular sets of social practices, such as practices that support access or practices that support meaning making, might mature and evolve.

Teaching as Strategic Work

Rather than walk away from what we have learned through years of literacy research because of various institutional mandates, it is important that we use what we have learned to evaluate and assess our current teaching practices in spite of these mandates. This evaluation calls for revisiting our teaching practices to consider how literacy has been constructed in different settings. We need to ask questions like, Who has access to our curriculum? In other words,

Does the curriculum support diverse learners?

Does the curriculum make use of learners' past experiences and their ways of talking about the world?

Does the curriculum make use of learners' past experiences and their ways of acting in and on the world?

Does the curriculum take into consideration topics and issues about which children are passionate?

We also need to find out what repertoires of literacy skills are made available to students through the work we do in our classrooms. We need to ask questions like,

> Are my literacy lessons focused primarily on phonics or spelling tests?
>
> Do my kids copy existing texts or do they imagine their own storylines?
>
> Do my kids read and write for real purposes?
>
> Do my kids have opportunities to create texts that have real-life functions and purposes and that make a difference in the real world?
>
> Do my kids engage in literacy work that repositions them in the world and in so doing lets them create alternate life trajectories for themselves?
>
> Do I take into consideration my students' understanding of technology and multiple media?
>
> Do I create spaces in my classroom for the everyday literacies and texts that my students bring to the classroom?

Further, we need to consider in what ways the curriculum advantages some students over other students. More specifically, we need to ask questions like,

> Do all my students have access to the resources needed to participate in the work we do in class?
>
> Are all my students able to participate equally?
>
> Do I take stock of the linguistic and cultural differences my students bring with them to the classroom?
>
> What literacies do I value?
>
> What literacies do I ignore or marginalize?

Asking these kinds of questions could be a way for teachers to be strategic in their teaching and consider what difference the practices they adopt in their classrooms has on students' acquisition of particular kinds of literacy. "If curriculum is a metaphor for the lives we want to live and the people we want to be, then we and our children need a framework that allows us to develop rich experiences and see the big picture when planning and living curriculum" (Egawa & Harste, 2001). A theoretical and pedagogical framework can create space for us to step back and consider the implications of the work we do from both a micro and a macro level. To this end, while considering theoretical and pedagogical frameworks for this book we decided to draw from the work of Luke and Freebody (1999), Janks (2002), and Egawa and Harste (2001).

Negotiating a Framework for This Book

Luke and Freebody's (1999) four resources model was the first tool we considered using as part of our conceptual framework for this book. The four resources model offered an opportunity for us to consider our teaching as a repertoire of practices that produce particular kinds of learners. For instance, one of the repertoires of practices Luke and Freebody discuss is helping children to analyze texts critically. By engaging in textual analysis in the classroom we shape our students to become critical readers of the world. The four resources model also helped us to look closely at our teaching practices to consider both theoretical and pedagogical gaps in the work we do with students.

The second model that informed our thinking while organizing this book was Hilary Janks's Synthesis Model for Critical Literacy (2002). Her model helped us to consider the relationship between language and power, particularly how our discursive practices (our ways of talking, doing, and being) privilege some of our students while disadvantaging others. Janks's model also reminded us that critical analysis is not enough. We also need to contribute to the shaping and design of our own futures.

The third model that we drew from while organizing this book was Egawa and Harste's "Halliday Plus" model for literacy learning (2001). Their model helped ground our work in the rich history of the language arts by outlining the elements they deem necessary in a good language arts program, namely: meaning making, language study, inquiry-based learning, and critical literacy.

In combination these frameworks and theoretical tools can assist teachers to "evaluate the scope and potential"(Wilson, 2002, p. 11) of their literacy program. We chose these tools in particular because they closely match our conceptualization of literacy as noted earlier in this chapter.

The "Four Resources" Model

One of the strengths of the "four resources model" is that it attempts to recognise and incorporate many of the current and well-developed techniques for training students in becoming literate. **It shifts the focus from trying to find the right method to whether the range of practices emphasised in one's reading program are indeed covering and integrating a broad repertoire of textual practices.** (Luke & Freebody, 1999; authors' emphasis)

While developing their model Luke and Freebody examined existing and proposed literacy curricula and pedagogical strategies. They state that effective literacy draws on a repertoire of practices that allow learners, as they engage in reading and writing activities, to participate in various "families of literate practices." They use the term "practices" to denote work done by literate beings in classrooms and beyond in everyday social contexts. In the Four Resources Model four dynamic and fluid families of social practices are described as necessary for literacy development.

Practices That Support Code Breaking

These practices refer to the skills required to break the code of language. For example, to break the code or understand the interplay between the complex bits and pieces that make up written texts requires recognizing and using the basic features and architecture of language, including the alphabet, sounds in words, spelling, and structural conventions and patterns. The more complex codes that we need to make sense of are broader cultural codes or discourses, that is, a community's ways of doing, talking, and acting.

Practices That Support Meaning Making

These practices involve participating in understanding and composing meaningful written, visual, and spoken texts, taking into account an individual's available knowledge and his or her experiences of other cultural discourses.

Practices That Support Using Texts

These practices involve using texts by knowing about and acting on the different cultural and social functions that various texts perform inside and outside school. Practices that support using texts also include understanding that the functions of texts shape the way they are structured, their tones, their degrees of formality, and their sequences of components.

Practices That Create Space for Critical Analysis

These practices involve the critical analysis and transformation of texts, based on the understanding that texts are ideologically charged and as such they represent particular points of view where some perspectives are silenced while other perspectives are privileged. These practices also operate on the belief that texts are socially constructed and therefore can be reconstructed. (From *Further Notes on the Four Resources Model* at www.readingonline.org/research/lukefreebody.html.)

Each family of practices is needed for literacy learning. Each of the four is inclusive, with each being integral to the achievement of the others.

Reflection Point

This is the first of a series of Reflection Points included throughout the book. They are meant to provide you with thoughtful questions and activities to help you make connections between ideas presented in this book and your own teaching practice.

Use the chart here, or re-create it in a journal, to jot down the different literate practices you make available in your classroom. In other words, what are the various engagements and activities that you use to support your students' growth in literacy?

Luke and Freebody's Four
Resources Model

Practices that support code breaking	Practices that support meaning making

Practices that support using texts	Practices that create space for critical analysis

Reflect on the following questions after filling out the Four Resources Model chart.

Were you able to come up with teaching practices for each of the four families of practice?

Which ones did you find challenging to fill in?

Do some practices dominate the literacy work you do?

What could you do to further develop strategies for engaging with the less frequently addressed families of practice?

A Synthesis Model for Critical Literacy

Critical literacy education is based on a socio-cultural theory of language and is particularly concerned with teaching learners to understand and manage the relationship between language and power. However, different realizations of critical literacy operate with different conceptions of this relationship by foregrounding domination, access, diversity or design. (Janks, 2002)

In her synthesis model for critical literacy, Janks argues that domination, access, diversity, and design are four orientations in critical literacy education that are crucially interdependent. She developed the model after realizing that there are different versions of critical literacy unfolding in different places and that each version has the tendency to highlight or foreground one of these orientations. This tendency, she notes, is problematic, as it limits our opportunities to understand how language works in powerful ways and therefore limits our opportunities to manage the relationship between language and power. Being unable to manage this relationship could result in , for example, privileging some students over others or privileging certain kinds or forms of knowledge over others.

Domination

According to Janks, theorists working from a view of power as domination see language, other symbolic forms, and discourse, more broadly, as a powerful means of maintaining and reproducing relations of domination. What this means is that there exist dominant ways of being, saying, and doing that are represented through multimodal texts that intersect our lives on a daily basis. These texts are never neutral. They are constructed and as such can be deconstructed in order to help us to understand "how language works to position readers in the interests of power" (Janks, 1993, p. iii).

Access

One way of doing this deconstruction is through Critical Language Awareness (CLA). Janks refers to CLA as pedagogy for engaging in critical discourse analysis (analyzing the relationship between language and power) by looking closely at and analyzing units of language (Janks, 2002, p. 4):

Critical Language Awareness emphasizes that anything that has been constructed can be de-constructed. This unmaking or unpicking of the text increases our awareness of the choices that the writer or speaker has made. Every choice foregrounds what was selected and hides, silences or backgrounds what was not selected. Awareness of this prepares the reader to ask critical questions: why did the writer or speaker make these choices? Whose interests do they serve? Who is empowered or disempowered by the language used? (Janks, 1993, p. iii)

Access   Access refers to making available dominant ways of doing, saying, and being while simultaneously valuing the linguistic and cultural diversity and the literacies of our students. Janks states, " If we provide students with access to dominant forms, this contributes to maintaining their dominance. If, on the other hand, we deny students access, we perpetuate their marginalization in a society that continues to recognize the value and importance of these forms" (2002, p. 5). The question then becomes how to make these dominant ways visible so that they are accessible to all students while at the same time valuing students' home literacies.

Diversity   According to Janks (2002), when a diverse group of students brings to the classroom different ways of reading and writing the world in a range of sign systems (music, art, writing), they bring with them a central resource for changing consciousness (the way we think about and operate in the world).

The challenge for us is to find ways to make education more inclusive of our students' diverse languages and literacies. Providing space in the classroom for these differences, according to Janks, "increases the creative resources that students can draw on" (p. 6).

Design   The design orientation deals with the notion of human creativity and the ability to generate new meanings using different semiotic systems across diverse cultural locations. In doing so the intent is to challenge and change dominant discourses or dominant ways of doing, acting, and speaking. (Janks, 2002)

For teachers this means we need to make different semiotic resources and sign systems available for our students so that they can construct meaning in transformative ways. Janks argues for the interdependence of domination, access, diversity, and design, arguing that "all of these orientations to literacy education are important and, moreover, that *they are crucially interdependent*. They should not be seen as separate enterprises." She continues by saying that "any one of domination, diversity, access or design without the others, creates a problematic imbalance" (2002, p. 6).

For more on the Synthesis Model for Critical Literacy refer to Janks (in press).

Reflection Point

Reflect on your teaching practice. Use the web in the chart on page xx to jot down how you see each of Janks's orientations—domination, access, diversity, and design—playing out in your classroom. Then draw arrows connecting each of the orientations that you feel work co-dependently.

Which orientations work independently in your classroom?
Which orientations work co-dependently?
How might you reconsider your practice to make sure that each of these orientations works interdependently?

Halliday Plus Model

Carolyn Burke says that the function of curriculum is to "give perspective," by which she means provide teachers and students with a bigger picture. Unfortunately, the current call for "balance" in the curriculum, regardless of its initial intent, fails to invite teachers to see the big picture. . . . Rather than walk away from what we know about language and learning, it is important that we incorporate such mandates into a bigger picture of what it means to be literate. (Egawa & Harste, 2001, p. 2)

To help us develop a bigger picture, Egawa and Harste (2001) suggest a framework for thinking about the effects our teaching practices have on our students. Their framework, which we have dubbed the "Halliday Plus" Model, consists of four components, which build on what we know from past research and experience about language learning. The Halliday Plus Model works from the belief that literacy is socially constructed. Said differently, the model builds on the idea that different teaching practices and different life experiences construct particular kinds of literate beings. As a result, different groups of people have different literacies that they use to negotiate their world. The difference between school literacy and outside-of-school literacies is simply that as educators we don't value the latter. Egawa and Harste argue that this attitude toward out-of-school literacy has to change. Rather than privilege one kind of literacy at the expense of other forms, we need to encourage critical as well as multiple literacies. A good language arts program for the twenty-first century therefore should comprise the following components: meaning making, language study, inquiry-based learning, and critical literacy, which they define as "learning to use language to critique" (see Figure 1).

Egawa and Harste's framework for thinking about the language arts curriculum is built upon Michael Halliday's insights on

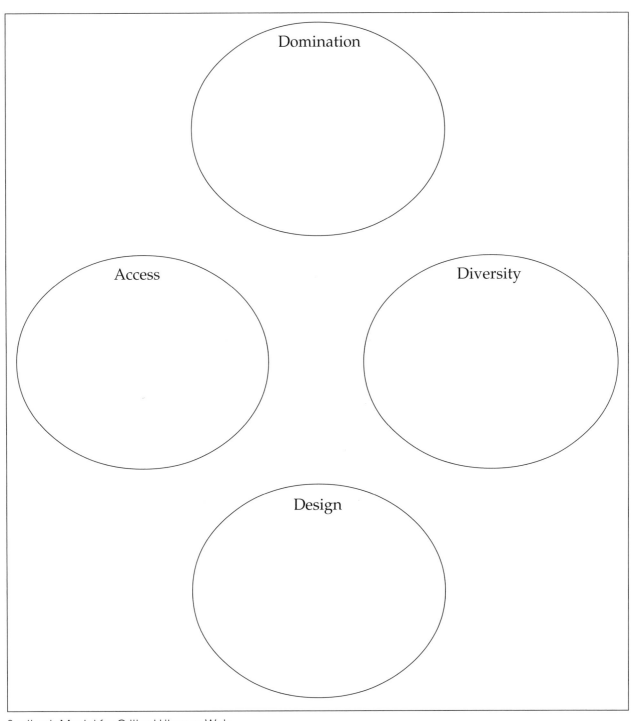

Synthesis Model for Critical Literacy Web

Figure 1.
Harste and Egawa's
Halliday Plus Model

Learning Language or Meaning Making	Learning about Language or Language Study
Using language and other sign systems as a meaning-making process, as during regularly scheduled read-aloud, partner reading with big books, readers' theater, or independent reading and writing engagements. Students might also keep journals, say something to a classmate about what they read, or symbolize in art what they think the story means.	Understanding how texts operate and how they are coded. This includes the teaching of letter-sound relationships and understanding how language works, as when introducing strategies that students might use in comprehending books, demonstrating how texts include some people while excluding others, or conducting a minilesson on how authors get texts to serve their purposes.
Examples: • Read-aloud • Shared reading • Partner reading • Readers' theater • Independent reading and writing • Writer's notebook • Big books • Journals • Reading log	**Examples:** • Strategy instruction • Demonstrations • Focused lessons • Minilessons • Class charts
Learning through Language or Inquiry-Based Learning	**Learning to Use Language to Critique or Critical Literacy**
Using reading and writing as tools and toys for learning about our world, as when teachers put together text sets that allow children to explore topics of personal interest, ask them to keep reflective journals, or support them in conducting focused studies centered on their own inquiry questions.	Using language to question what seems normal and natural, as well as to redesign and create alternate social worlds, as when teachers create spaces in their classrooms for conversations about social issues or invite children to interrogate the Internet, media, advertisements, and other everyday texts.
Examples: • Literature study • Inquiry or focus studies • Reflective journals • Sketch to Stretch • Say Something • Process drama	**Examples:** • Books that support critical conversations • Community-action projects • Interrogating everyday texts • Audit Trail or Learning Wall showing important social issues addressed over time

how language is learned (1975). One of Halliday's major insights into language learning was that children "learn language," "learn about language," and "learn through language" simultaneously. Every encounter with language therefore provides the learner with an opportunity to learn how to use language to make sense or to mean (what we call "meaning making" and Halliday called "learning language");

learn about language as a linguistic object, e.g., that it is composed of letter-sound relationships or that word order makes a difference (what we call "language study" and what Halliday called "learning about language"); and

learn more about their world, that is, get smarter (what we refer to as "inquiry-based learning" and what Halliday called "learning through language").

Egawa and Harste cast Halliday's thinking as a framework for rethinking the language arts curriculum by elaborating on the kinds of curricular invitations and engagements teachers might provide their students. Their intent is to encourage teachers to consider how they might organize their language arts classroom for purposes of creating a critically literate human being for the twenty-first century.

Reflection Point

> Using a highlighter pen and the chart in Figure 1, which explains the Halliday Plus Model, highlight all of the curricular engagements you already have in place in your classroom. Select one of the things not highlighted to implement. Think through what social practices you will need to engage in and what social practices you hope to see in your students. To keep your focus on "the big picture," think through what implementing that engagement on a regular basis would mean in terms of the kinds of literate being you are creating.

How This Book Is Organized

Each of the models previously described—Luke and Freebody's Four Resources Model, Janks's Synthesis Model for Critical Literacy, and Egawa and Harste's Halliday Plus Model—informed our thinking about the kinds of teaching practices we ought to encourage in classrooms. While looking across the three as frameworks we came up with four sets of classroom practices that we decided to use for organizing this book. They are practices that support access, practices that support meaning making, practices that support inquiry, and practices that support transformation.

Practices That Support Access

Access should be about exploring with children how language is coded well beyond the word. For most educators today "breaking the code" means teaching children about phonics or the study of graphophonemic patterns ("rhyme and theme" if you want to be really hip). For some teachers, "breaking the code" might include comprehension and more specifically strategy instruction, by which they usually mean the systematic introduction of things proficient readers do to make sense of text. Rarely, however, does "breaking the code" go beyond strategy instruction in comprehension.

The articles included in this section were chosen as examples of the kinds of work done by teachers in the area of code breaking. Further, they are included to create space for you to think about ways of reimagining what it means to break broader sociocultural codes through unpacking not only the "word" but also the "world" (Freire, 1970), that is, to consider the ways in which we make sense of the world around us where discourses (ways of doing, talking, and being) are at times conflicting and at other times complementary.

Practices That Support Meaning Making

We have learned a good deal about the role that language plays in meaning making, and in some cases even created powerful new instructional strategies based on these understandings. We have also learned that new literacies are not only print literacies. More than likely they are multimodal (taking different forms such as books and newspaper articles) and multimedial (combining different means of communication such as the Internet, DVDs, and music) literacies (Sefton-Greene, 2001). In some ways the future should be about opening up the canon in order to expand our definition of literacy and include all of the ways we have at our disposal to mean (art, music, drama, movement, language). However, new forms of literacy will need to be studied in terms of the social practices they encourage, including information and communication technologies such as cell phones, the Internet, music videos, and video billboards. In this section we included articles that create space for discussing ways that educators might experiment with alternate literacies and alternate social practices to propel new learning.

Practices That Support Inquiry

In our experience most reading and language arts programs in the United States highlight meaning making and code breaking. For most people, these two components make up a language arts program. Over the years we have continued to argue that in addition to meaning making and code breaking, children need lots of opportunities to use reading and writing to learn. Children in the twenty-first century have few guarantees. The only thing we can be sure of is that they will face problems of some magnitude, including resource shortages, pollution, homelessness, and poverty, and the list goes on. Given this likelihood, it follows that to prepare children for the twenty-first century we need to make them problem solvers. Further, since no single person is going to be able to solve problems of this magnitude, children are going to have to know how to inquire together. This, in a nutshell, is what education as inquiry is all about. The articles included in this section were included to set up a discussion on practices that support social and collaborative inquiry.

Practices That Support Transformation

A female colleague once said to Harste that it was not enough that he "understood" women's liberation, he now had to "act differently," too. Too often in schools we study subjects, ticking them off (chemistry, physics, earth science, etcetera) as if somehow we are done with them the day we walk out of class. Instead of perpetuating such social practices, it is important to aim higher. Social action ought to be one outcome of learning. The key question we need to help our children ask themselves is, How am I going to reposition myself in the world? For instance, how am I going to act differently? Or how am I going to talk differently?

Together teachers and children need to explore how making social statements and taking social action can become part of everyday life in twenty-first-century classrooms. The articles included in this section provide demonstrations of work done by classroom teachers engaged in this work.

Reflection Points and Resource Boxes

Throughout the book you will find "reflection points" and "resource boxes." The use of reflection points was discussed earlier in this chapter. We see reflection and action as an integral part of being a teacher, that is, using what we have learned from observing what our teaching practices have produced to consider other ways of teaching. Therefore, in each section of the book you will find reflection points to create spaces for you to interact with this text and/or to begin discussions about literacy teaching and learning with colleagues. These points for reflection will take a variety of forms, including questions to spark your thinking about a certain theme, concept, strategy, or topic. Other points for reflection include looking closely and analyzing children's talk or artifacts of children's learning such as writing samples. Reflection points could also take the form of suggesting strategies to try in the classroom followed by writing a journal entry. You will also find various resource boxes throughout the book. These boxes are meant to provide you with additional resources for exploring particular topics, ideas, or constructs.

The final part of the book is a forward-looking section that sets up a conversation regarding possible educational futures as seen from the perspective of literacy as social practice.

Reflection Point

As a way of beginning to read this book we invite you to use the social practices chart to list the social practices you already have going on in your classroom that support access, meaning making, inquiry, and transformation. Then reflect on what new social practices you wish to engage in with your students.

Social Practices Chart

Social practices I currently engage in with my students that support access	Social practices I currently engage in with my students that support meaning making
Social practices I currently engage in with my students that support inquiry	**Social practices I currently engage in with my students that support transformation**

References   Dole, J. A., & Osborn, J. (2003). Elementary language arts textbooks: A decade of change. In J. Flood (Ed.), *Handbook of research on teaching the English language arts* (2nd ed., pp. 631–639). Mahwah, NJ: Erlbaum.

Egawa, K., & Harste, J. C. (2001). Balancing the literacy curriculum: A new vision. *School Talk, 7*(1).

Freire, P. (1970). *Pedagogy of the oppressed* (Ramos, M. B., Trans.). New York: Continuum.

Graves, M. F. (1998, October/November). Forum: Beyond balance. *Reading Today, 16,* 16.

Halliday, M. A. K. (1975). *Learning how to mean: Explorations in the development of language.* London: Arnold.

Janks, H. (1993). *Language, identity and power.* Johannesburg: Hodder.

Janks, H. (2002, November). *Synthesis model for critical literacy.* Paper presented at the NCTE Annual Convention, Atlanta, GA.

Janks, H. (in press). Methods, models, and motivations. In V. Vasquez and J. C. Harste (Eds.), *Keynoting critical literacies.* Newark, DE: International Reading Association.

Luke, A., & Freebody, P. (1999). A map of possible practices: Further notes on the four resources model [Electronic version]. *Practically Primary, 4*(2), 5–8. Retrieved June 28, 2004, from www.alea.edu.au/freebody.htm.

Myers, M. (1996). *Changing our minds: Negotiating English and literacy.* Urbana, IL: National Council of Teachers of English.

Rosenblatt, L. (2003). Literary theory. In J. Flood (Ed.), *Handbook of research on teaching the English language arts* (2nd ed., pp. 67–73). Mahwah, NJ: Erlbaum.

Sefton-Greene, J. (2001). The "end of school" or just "out of school"? ICT, the home and digital cultures. In C. Durrant & C. Beavis, *P(ICT)ures of English: Teachers, learners and technology.* Kent Town, S. Australia: Wakefield Press.

Smith, K., & Lambert Stock, P. (2003). Trends and issues in research in the teaching of the English language arts. In J. Flood (Ed.), *Handbook of research on teaching the English language arts* (2nd ed., pp. 114–132). Mahwah, NJ: Erlbaum.

Squire, J. R. (2003). The history of the profession. In J. Flood (Ed.), *Handbook of research on teaching the English language arts* (2nd ed., pp. 3–17). Mahwah, NJ: Erlbaum

Vasquez, V., & Harste, J. C. (Eds.). (in press). *Keynoting critical literacies.* Newark, DE: International Reading Association.

Wilson, L. (2002). *Reading to live: How to teach reading for today's world.* Portsmouth, NH: Heinemann.

I Practices That Support Access

Language is coded way beyond letter-sound relationships. That being the case, we need to help our students understand the different ways language is coded in order to make language truly accessible for them. For instance, we need to help them understand both syntax, the flow of language or word order, and semantics, word choice or lexicogrammatical choices. M. A. K. Halliday, in *Learning How to Mean: Explorations in the Development of Language* (London: Edward Arnold, 1975), says that every instance of language signs its context. For instance, the phrase "Railroad Strike Averted," he says, is clearly a piece of written text; one you would find in a newspaper or on the screen of your favorite news program. The phrase "Get ready, get set, go" is oral language. The language itself signals the setting in which such a phrase is found. In addition to the mode of communication, oral language, we know what kinds of activities are occurring, as well as the social relationship of the participants involved to one another. Halliday calls these dimensions of language, the field, the mode, and the tenor. The word *FIRE* is a complete text, he argues, for which we can imply a context.

Semantically, J. P. Gee argues in *What Video Games Have to Teach Us about Learning and Literacy* (New York: Palgrave, 2003) that every piece of language has a cultural model. For him, cultural models are frames of reference that language users conjure up as they try to understand the meaning of a particular text. What are some ways that we can help our students to break the code or understand how frames of reference operate as they negotiate meaning in the world?

To be literate in the twenty-first century requires an understanding of how language is coded beyond phonics. For instance, we also need to understand how language operates semantically, socioculturally, and syntactically in order to understand how language positions us in the world. That is, how does language work in powerful ways to advantage and privilege some while disadvantaging and marginalizing others?

Each of the articles included in this section focuses on ways that teachers and students together explore breaking various codes of language; they specifically deal with the fundamental features and architecture of language, including the alphabet, sounds in words, conventions of language, patterns and sentence structure, and spelling. Your role as reader will be to imagine what other codes the students and teachers in the articles could work on understanding. More specifically, what are some ways that the teachers in the articles can make language and literacy learning more accessible to their students?

The articles included in this section are "Learning with Jaime," by D. Yoshizawa, "Talk during One-on-One Interactions," by S. Forsyth, R. Forbes, S. Scheitler, and M. Schwade, and "Driven to Read," by C. Kawamoto.

Learning with Jaime

Dianne Yoshizawa

In the first article, "Learning with Jaime," first-grade teacher Dianne Yoshizawa writes about her experience using a hypothesis test form while working with Jaime, one of her students. She used this evaluation tool first to get to know him and then to figure out how to support him in learning some basic language structures such as directionality in drawing and language patterns in writing and reading. Eventually, through ongoing observation, she discovered ways of making language learning more accessible for Jaime.

The "hypothesis test" process is an inquiry-based assessment tool developed by Diane Stephens and colleagues, with the collaboration of teacher-researchers, to help struggling learners to improve in literacy growth and development. The cyclical reflective steps include "observing behavior, interpreting why behavior exists, figuring out possible hypotheses, and making curricular decisions." For more on the hypothesis test process refer to D. Stephens and J. Story, Assessment as Inquiry: Learning the Hypothesis-Test Process *(Urbana, IL: NCTE, 1999).*

Jaime has been my student the last two years, first for kindergarten, and then again when I switched to first grade. I first met Jaime when he and his family took advantage of the half hour I schedule for each kindergartner to come and explore the classroom with his family before the new school year begins. Sometimes older brothers and sisters will come, often to show off their former room. This gives the kindergartner an opportunity to explore new grounds in comfortable company. Jaime came with his younger sister and brother, an older sister who enjoys coming to the kindergarten room, and his mother and father.

I invited the whole family to sign in on a half sheet of chart paper and write whatever else they wanted to with markers. Jaime whispered to Mom, "I don't know how." His sisters and brother excitedly picked up the pen and started to write while Mom was assuring Jaime that he could do it. Jaime very hesitantly wrote a "J" and scribbled little squiggly lines after it.

My next meeting with Jaime was on the first day of school. I invited Jaime and all of the kindergartners and their families into the classroom. Jaime cautiously entered the room. He walked in as if he had never been there before, holding his mother's hand and looking at me with big quiet eyes. It wasn't that same little romping, jumping

From *Primary Voices K–6, 5*(1), Jan. 1997, 18–23.

kindergartner who covered the chalkboard with drawings and writings, or the Jaime who was enjoying himself in the living center the day before. As in our first meeting, I asked him to write his name on the big chart paper and again he softly muttered in a whispering voice, "I don't know how." Despite his discomfort, he picked up a marker and wrote a "J." He looked at Mom who said, "Go on, you're doing okay," and Jaime followed the "J" with many squiggly little lines.

"I don't know how" were Jaime's whispered words every time something new was introduced. Despite the tension of the "I don't know how" that morning, from that day on he frequently chose to go to the chalkboard to practice writing his name independently. Every so often I felt a little tug on my dress and there was Jaime pointing to the chalkboard and showing me the change that was occurring in the writing. Occasionally, he asked me to join in these celebrations. Besides celebrating his accomplishments in writing, Jaime continuously asked me to read different books to him. I often called others to join us so we could be in a little group with Jaime.

In the middle of the second day of school, some of the children were busy playing with the blocks, and others were engaged in reading and writing. On the far end of the room, I spotted Jaime quietly looking at everyone with big sad eyes and droopy shoulders. I walked to him and asked, "What's the matter, Jaime?" Two great big tears welled from his eyes and slowly rolled down his cheeks. "What's happening, Jaime?" I asked. "I don't want to be here by myself," he cried softly. I thought to myself, "You have all the other boys and girls. So many other children and you're saying, 'I'm by myself?'"

Many more times I saw and wrote about Jaime on the floor by himself. He'd be writing, reading, playing blocks, working on a puzzle, but he was always by himself on the floor. Jaime with his family and Jaime in the classroom presented two contrasting pictures. Each day, after his family left, he was the quiet Jaime who chose to be by himself. He looked at the others from far away but didn't join them. If he were involved with others, he was always on the fringes of the group, looking in but not deeply engaged. I couldn't forget those big quiet teary eyes those first few days of school.

The picture made Jaime seem almost fragile. How was he going to learn if he continued to say, "I don't know how" and kept to himself? How could I help him? Learning is risk taking and a social process. How was this going to happen with Jaime? I needed time to find the Jaime that laughed and ran with his brothers and sisters. The Engagements group was an ideal way for me to get to know Jaime.

"Jaime, tomorrow I'll have time to be with you in the library. What would you like to do?" I asked Jaime the day before our session. "Play with blocks, read books, and draw," said Jaime. He clearly formed our agenda for the first session and the others that followed. He knew what he wanted to do.

As we walked into the library, Jaime's eyes surveyed the stacks of books in the library with awe, so we headed to the shelves and Jaime pulled off *One Fish, Two Fish, Red Fish, Blue Fish* (1960/1987) by Dr. Seuss. "I have this at home but it's torn," said Jaime. We pulled the book out, sprawled out between the stacks, and began reading. Jaime began by pointing and reading the title with me. As I read, he continuously commented on the book. When he saw the line of animals and creatures, he looked for the "worm." Then he saw the big cat and said, "Cat in the Hat."

When he saw the camel with many humps, he sang the camel song and said it was from Barney. I was amazed at how much Jaime talked. When Jaime saw all the colored fishes in Dr. Seuss's book, he related that to the Power Rangers and their colors. What a different Jaime! We even dramatized the different actions of the Power Rangers because Jaime wanted to draw them. I noticed, however, that the feet in his figures were turning in all directions, not anchored to a baseline. The feet were up, down, and sideways.

As part of the Engagement session, we teachers spent several hours talking about what happened in our sessions, reflecting, problem solving, and collaborating. "Take a few minutes to write a detailed minute-by-minute account of how you picked up your student at the classroom. What did you say to him as you walked with him to the library? How did you inform him of the sessions? How did you decide where to work in the Engagement work area? How did you decide what to do and how to set up the materials you were working with?" said Diane, a few minutes into our meeting time. I was beginning to understand that thinking through and reflecting on these little moments would help me to understand Jaime and establish that highly literate relationship with him. Whatever I did could affect our relationship. Each moment and interaction was a very important occurrence; nothing ought to be overlooked. What a powerful role I had!

To learn from my sessions with Jaime, I logged my Observations, made multiple Interpretations, Hypothesized under what conditions certain experiences were occurring or could possibly occur, made some Curricular Decisions based on these Hypotheses, and reflected on the total process. Fortunately, Jaime was a pupil in my class, so the Hypotheses could be tested in the classroom as Jaime engaged in a regular school day. This was an ongoing process for me. One way for me to analyze our relationship was by writing and reflecting on my experiences with Jaime.

Although I didn't start working one-on-one with Jaime until January, many of the Observations I had made in the classroom setting in the fall supported my decision making in the HT process as I learned it:

> 10/13 After reading a story, many children wanted to draw rabbits; Jaime said he didn't know how. We talked about what a rabbit has. Each time we mentioned a part, Jaime drew it. Pretty soon, he had his rabbit. Next couple of writings, he wanted to draw rabbits.

> 10/14 Jaime shared a book he had written. He was sharing it upside down until the others told him. He turned it right side up easily, but later shared it upside down again. Mom expressed concern about his drawing. I told her how we did the rabbit and she talked him through a detailed fire truck.

After my first Engagements session with Jaime, as I wrote and thought about our encounter, I listed 18 Observations about Jaime and tried to propose at least 5 possible Interpretations for each one; in some cases, I needed to go back and write some additional Interpretations. Figure 1.1 shows 5 examples.

At our next session, Jaime chose the same table to work at. We brought blocks and the books we hadn't read the previous week. Figure 1.2 contains excerpts from my HT sheets for that session, January 26.

On February 2, we started with our blocks and some zoo animals that I was going to introduce to the class since we had visited the zoo. We constructed a zoo and Jaime and I categorized the animals into caged and grazing animals. This happened because I asked Jaime where was he going to put the animals. Were they all going to be together? Jaime said that the lion, tiger, and cheetah need to be in cages by themselves because they might eat the other animals. We also separated the elephant because he might hurt someone with his trunk or big heavy legs. Jaime also said to put the gorilla in a cage by himself, for he might throw things and hurt others. We placed the giraffe and the camel to graze, along with the rhinoceros. Then we each chose an animal to draw. He chose the lion and I chose the giraffe. Since we were talking about the lion, I decided to draw a lion too. We looked at the lion and talked about his mane, the head, the hair on the body, and his strong legs. Then we each drew our lion as we had talked about it. When I was finished, Jaime said, "I thought you were going to draw a giraffe." I asked him, "Do you want me to draw a giraffe?" He nodded, so I began

Figure 1.1.
Examples of Observations
and Possible Interpretations

1. Jaime told me he wanted to read books, draw, and play blocks when I told him he and I would be working together.
    a. seems to like what we do in class
    b. doesn't know what else to do
    c. has a sense of what he wants to do
    d. seems to be able to make a choice when asked to
    e. only knows what I have laid out in the classroom

3. He pointed and read with me as I read the title.
    f. very familiar with the book
    g. loves the book
    h. knows this book well
    i. very interactive in reading process
    j. likes reading process

8. We spent a long time drawing Power Rangers.
    a. very interested in topic
    b. likes drawing
    c. drawing Power Rangers is safe
    d. drawing and talking is okay for him
    e. engages in what he is interested in

11. Jaime drew the head and then intersected a bigger circle and said it was the body. The "body" circle was positioned on all points of the circle head. Mostly above.
    a. sense of grounding didn't concern him
    b. does not understand that directionality is meaningful
    c. ?
    d. ?
    e. ?

12. He named each character, so I asked him to write their names so I could remember, too. His first response was, "I don't know how."
    a. writing is not in his comfortable zone
    b. lacks confidence
    c. thinks it has to be right
    d. reluctant to take risks
    e. ?

drawing the giraffe with the same kind of conversation we had about the lion. What do I see? I see the long neck, the small head, I see the ears and the two small horns of the head. After talking about the animal, I began to draw. As I drew, Jaime reminded me of the parts I needed to draw.

When I said, "Let's write a story about our drawing," Jaime said, "I don't know how." I hadn't heard that from Jaime for a long time. Then he said, "You write." I said "Okay," and wrote *lion*. He

Hypothesis-Test Sheet

Name: Jaime
Teacher: Dianne Yoshizawa

Observations	Interpretations	Hypotheses	Curricular Decisions
3. Jaime built structures that went up and said he was building a "longer" house. (I used the term "taller" and soon he was using that term too.) 5. He built level structures which were very long. He called them "trains" and he tried to push the narrow block through the holes that ran through the long trains. It took him time to figure out that he had to align the holes so that it would connect into one long tunnel. He could connect it with three or four blocks but had not figured out how to align them when they were longer. 6. Jaime and I copied the movements of the Power Rangers. It took him time to figure out my position and copy me. 9. When he couldn't push the "train block car" through the long tunnel, he removed each block as the block car went through the tunnel.	3a. Terminology for directionality not defined. 3b. Open to learning terminology 3c. Understands comparative terms; e.g., *longer*. 5a. The longer it is, the more aligning takes place. 5b. He has not seen the hole as it runs through. 5c. He has not figured out that the blocks on the outside will help with the aligning on the inside. 5d. He cannot visualize what he has not seen. 5e. He does not seem to see the pattern. 6a. Seemed to like dramatizing. 6b. Copying, mirroring seems to take figuring out. 6c. Mirroring seemed to be an easier task than copying on paper. 6d. Drawing is more abstract than mirroring. 6e. Seemed relaxed with dramatizing and drawing, even if the tasks took time. 9a. Solves problems in his own ways. 9b. Problem solving very nonchalantly approached. 9c. His perception of what needs to be done and mine are very different. 9d. I thought he was trying to make a long tunnel. The length of the tunnel did not matter. He just seemed to be satisfied that the train was moving along. 9e. Playing building gives space for Jaime's decisions.	When situations are okay, or safe, he seems to function more as he functions with his family. If that is so, then he needs the safe environment so he can play and engage. The safety will come from our personal interaction and the time we build together. Has some difficulty with spatial relationships. Jaime really likes writing, and I think dramatizing and getting a sense of his body and his position will eventually help him transfer to the abstract of writing letters. Right now he will use letters of his name for that is what he is familiar with. As he works with his body and space in concrete ways, he will record them in writing in this way.	I'll take time for the two of us to build this trusting relationship. I guess that's why I selected him. I just want more time with him so we can build safety together and venture together into the classroom. We'll put all these together at one time and let him engage and make meaning in any combination. We'll continue working in the areas of block building, reading— shark books for nonfiction and whatever fiction he chooses— dramatizing, and writing. I seem to be looking for ways that will open space for Jaime's recording in writing of what he sees since he lacked confidence in the beginning, but he has pushed himself strongly in this area.

Figure 1.2. Hypothesis Test Sheet for Jaime

picked up his pencil and wrote the same thing. "Jaime, you can write," I said. Then he wrote, "I saw the lion at the zoo." He was using little closed shapes to place hold his writing.

After that session, it was time to write a report for Jaime's parents. Working through the report of all the progress I had made with Jaime made me wonder if it was time to go on to another child, for I thought I knew my direction with Jaime. I was Pretty Sure I understood him as a learner: I believed that he needed to build relationships with people, that he was challenged by spatial relations, and that he needed more understanding of print and needed to gain control of print. However, in a conversation with Diane Stephens, she told me, "You seem to have arrived at some Pretty Sures, but where will you go from here?" She made me realize that I knew my direction but that I had to ask, "What was I going to do about it?" It was time to move to instruction, to build with Jaime.

As I worked with Jaime through the spring, I used my Pretty Sures to organize my Curricular Decisions for him in both our tutoring sessions and in the classroom. In both settings, I offered Jaime invitations that were designed to allow him to grow in these areas. Jaime had excellent relationships with his parents and siblings. To build on his ability to form relationships, I arranged for Jaime to work in tutoring pairs with the other teacher-student pairs in my Engagements group. In the classroom, I made sure that I supported flexible, changing working groups in which Jaime was welcomed as a contributing member. While I engaged all my children in experiments with print by inviting responses to wordless books, supporting invented spelling, and encouraging children to read and write about their interests, I paid special attention to Jaime as he began to write with letters instead of his block symbols and to take risks with his attempts at spelling. Realizing that all children could benefit from what I had learned from Jaime, I made more opportunities for the children to develop their perceptions about space, directionality, and proportion, offering opportunities for all of my children to explore materials and experiences with architecture, art, and movement. During our one-on-one sessions, Jaime and I continued to work with the concrete, such as clay, bubbles, and toys; we moved into predictable books, building on his successes, and continued writing and drawing.

By April, Jaime was confidently reading predictable books, finding writing strategies for himself, and engaging with other children as he would with me, using hand motions and his eyes. Jaime still continued to say, "I don't know how," whenever a new situation arose, but he engaged and persisted. His "I don't know how" eventually turned more positive through his own perseverance. He never said, "I don't want to, or I cannot." There always seemed to be hesitancy, but never a refusal.

As I look back on Jaime's growth during his kindergarten year, I am convinced that it was the multiple Interpretations for the Observations in the HT process that helped me give Jaime space to think, to use his voice to make connections, and to grow. My stepping back to watch for multiple Interpretations gave Jaime time and opportunity to make his own decisions, too. This year Jaime is in first grade and because of HT, I find myself observing and thinking why Jaime does what he does more than directing him to do it my way. I also find myself asking Jaime to think through his actions so that we can name his actions and value them. I am finding that what may be seen as a faltering or a mistake is really a miscue.

This past fall, I asked my students to attend parent-teacher conferences with their parents. I asked them to choose books they were able to read to their parents, and when miscues occurred, the parents, student, and I talked. As Jaime, now a first grader, read *When Itchy Witchy Sneezes* (1989) to his parents, he read the right-hand page before the left. Then he turned the page, stopped, turned the pages back again, carefully studied the two pages, and corrected himself. As his parents and I listened and watched, I asked Jaime what made him stop and change. He explained that he was looking at the sequence of the pictures and realized that they were not in the order he had read. Jaime's father said, "Whew, Jaime, you're a thinker! That's great!" I had used this opportunity to help Jaime name and reiterate the semantic cueing strategy of using the pictures to help with the reading and at the same time help his parents value Jaime's thinking. By walking Jaime through his own thinking process, we were able to see the importance of giving Jaime the time and the space to think, rather than jumping in and correcting him. Jaime helped me see the value of giving students the time and space to use their own voices to make connections.

Lingering Questions

Giving Jaime space to think, wonder, and wander has helped me to see how curriculum can grow and evolve from a student's interests. Seeing from multiple perspectives gives all children and learners space to grow, but it hasn't been easy for me. I am still wondering:

1. Will I be able to give all learners the space I've given Jaime?
2. How can I give them space when my agenda and the department agenda are so pressing?
3. Am I offering invitations to encourage intentions, organization, and experimentation, or am I pushing my own agenda?

4. Can I learn from my students in the classroom as I've learned from Jaime?

5. Can I continue to learn and persevere the way Jaime does?

References   Cowley, J. (1989). *When Itchy Witchy sneezes*. Bothell, WA: Wright Group.

Seuss, Dr. (1987). *One fish, two fish, red fish, blue fish*. New York: Random. (Originally published 1960.)

Stephens, D., and Story, J. (1999). *Assessment as inquiry: learning the hypothesis-test process*. Urbana, IL: NCTE.

Reflection Point

In this article we were privy to Dianne Yoshizawa's struggles in attempting to support Jaime's literacy growth. Through the use of an HT observation form she was able to understand the tensions Jaime was experiencing as he attempted to work at breaking the codes of language in order to read and write. To make literacy learning more accessible to Jaime, Dianne offered him multimodal opportunities, providing time and space for him to explore materials and experiences with architecture, art, and movement as a way of making sense of the process of reading and writing. She also understood that he needed to build relationships with people, another code he needed to break, in order to grow as a literate person.

Use the Hypothesis Test form in Resource Box 1 to observe a learner in your setting. Consider how you might use it as a tool for understanding how to make literacy learning more accessible for your student.

Resource Box 1

Hypothesis Test Sheet

Name: Date:
Teacher:

Observations	Interpretations	Hypotheses	Curricular Decisions

Talk during One-on-One Interactions

Sylvia Forsyth, Rosalie Forbes, Susan Scheitler, and
Marcia Schwade

The authors discuss the use of one-on-one interactions as a strategy for helping learners to understand how language works. For example, they talk about Natasha, a first grader, as she learned to make print-to-word matches in text and her classmate Jake who was learning strategies for retelling. They help their students experience and learn to understand their own active role in meaning making as they interact with the teacher and the text, and reflect on their own reading processes. In each case, specific cueing and prompting is based on a sound professional understanding of each student's needs. This professional decision making and application into practice supports what Luke and Freebody ("Further Notes on the Four Resources Model," Practically Primary, 1, *1999, 99) espouse when they say that with different students, different teaching approaches work differentially.*

When teachers hear their words echoed in the classroom and see students mimic their behaviors, they know that what they say and do during instruction strongly influences what learners learn. Clear and explicit teacher talk is powerful. Our study of teachers' instructional interactions suggests that expert teachers consciously and deliberately ensure the clarity of their instructional talk. They set appropriate learning goals and state them in language that is clear to students. They carefully scaffold students' active engagement in learning through explicit modeling, explanations, prompts, and cues. They give students specific feedback and guide students' reflections on their own actions to promote an awareness and control in learning. Teacher talk that is clear and explicit empowers learners, especially struggling readers and writers.

In this article, four of us share examples of explicit teacher talk to demonstrate its influence on learners. Rosalie and Sylvia describe teacher talk that promotes struggling readers' understandings and control in reading. Susan shows us that explicit modeling also empowers novice teachers, which in turn empowers students. Finally, Marcia demonstrates that clear instruction enables children to influence learning in peers.

From *Primary Voices K–6, 7*(1), Aug. 1998, 9–16.

Changing Reading Behaviors

When Rosalie worked with Natasha in a Reading Recovery program, she was pleased with her reading progress during the first few months of instruction. Natasha learned to make print-to-word matches in text and she knew how to reread to search for information. She learned to monitor her reading for meaning and could self-correct her reading errors. Her reading was fluent, phrased, and expressive. Natasha had advanced from reading books with only two or three words per page (readiness level) to books with several lines of print on each page (preprimer 3 level). In the more difficult texts, she consistently applied her reading strategies and continued her fluent reading.

Around the end of the eighth instructional week, Natasha's reading changed. Probably as a result of her reading minilessons and her experiences with writing text, Natasha began to focus on graphophonic cues (letter-to-sound relationships) in words. However, her attempts to sound out words rarely achieved success and her word-by-word reading slowed down her reading processes. She neglected the meaning and language cues she had previously used to problem-solve in text. Because she stopped to sound out each word, her reading was slow and dysfluent. She no longer predicted upcoming words and phrases and she did not reread to search for information.

Several factors indicated that Natasha was ready to handle the challenges of more difficult texts. She could read and write many known words in both context and isolation. She could easily write new words with familiar spelling patterns. Her accuracy rate in the more challenging texts was 90 percent or better at all times. All of these indicators suggested to Rosalie that more difficult books were appropriate for Natasha's instructional reading level.

Rosalie concluded that Natasha needed to reexperience fluency in reading in these more difficult texts. She thus decided to model fluent reading for and with Natasha. Rosalie carefully chose two books from the Rigby PM collection: *Baby Bear Goes Fishing* (Randall, 1996) and *The Hungry Kitten* (Randall, 1996). These books promote fluent reading since they have predictable language patterns and strong story lines. In addition, both books have more than one line of text on each page so that page turning does not frequently interrupt fluency. Natasha had previously read, but not memorized, both of these books, so solving word problems was not a major issue.

Rosalie succinctly and clearly explained her instruction to Natasha. She said, "I am going to read this book to you. I want you to listen to how I read it. Then I want you to read it just like I do." Then, she fluently read the entire book *Baby Bear Goes Fishing* for Natasha. She next invited Natasha to read along with her. When they finished choral reading, she asked Natasha to read the book by herself. Natasha's independent reading was fluent, expressive, and phrased.

Rosalie repeated this instructional sequence with *The Hungry Kitten*. After modeling fluent reading for and with Natasha, she let her try reading the book on her own. Again, Natasha's independent reading in this book was fluent.

Rosalie then asked Natasha to independently read an unfamiliar text, *Baby Bear's Present* (Randall, 1996). She told her to read this new text "just like you read the other two books." Natasha read her new book expressively and fluently. Reading fluently focused Natasha's attention to the meaning of text, and she could successfully use a variety of reading strategies to solve problems. She predicted unknown words using context cues and quickly checked her predictions with graphophonic information. She reread phrases and searched for information to self-correct her reading miscues. In just one lesson, Rosalie's clear and explicit modeling communicated powerfully to Natasha how to read fluently and enjoy fluent reading.

Building Metacognition

Sylvia analyzed Cathy Roller's instructional interactions with Alison during their one-to-one reading conferences (Forsyth, 1997). Here, she describes how Cathy's explicit feedback and guided reflections helped Alison build metacognitive awareness and control of her reading processes.

Alison had made good progress in learning to read. She could choose books that supported her level of reading and she effectively used her independent time to practice reading in a variety of texts. She had acquired some reading strategies that enabled her to solve problems in text, but she didn't always apply them. When she made meaning-changing reading errors, she often just kept right on reading. Cathy wanted Alison to gain further control of her reading processes by learning how to self-monitor her reading for meaning. The dialogues in Figure 2.1 are excerpted from a set of Cathy and Alison's reading conferences that occurred over several weeks as Cathy worked toward this goal.

In their first reading conference (June 26), Alison self-corrected a reading miscue as she read aloud from *Silly Sally* (Wood, 1992). Cathy took advantage of Alison's successful problem solving to draw her attention to new reading knowledge that Cathy wanted her to learn. Cathy gave Alison immediate feedback to reinforce her self-correcting behaviors and to highlight the importance of making meaning in text.

In a later conference (July 10), when Alison hesitated for several seconds before correctly identifying the word *catching*, Cathy

Figure 2.1.
Transcription of One-on-One
Interaction

Dialogue Key

asterisk *	pause of one second per asterisk
bold type	child's self-correction
[brackets]	actual text words
ellipsis . . .	interruption
italics	child's reading of text
(parentheses)	added explanation
plain type	conversation
underlining	overlapping speech

Alison Learns to Monitor Her Reading

June 26

Alison: *Now she did* * **Now how did** *Sally get to town?*

Cathy: You know you did a nice thing there. It wasn't making sense to you and you went back and corrected. Very good.

July 10

Cathy: How did you get *catching?*

Alison: I sounded it out.

Cathy: You sounded it out. Did you use the meaning? Did you try to make it make sense? 'Cause the meaning can really help you.

July 16

Cathy: How did you get *ducked?* Can you explain it to me?

Alison: Ducked? First, I sounded it out, then I knew it didn't make sense. Then I just got *ducked*. It made sense.

Cathy: Okay, so you tried *ducked* and it made sense. You were looking for the sense and you used the sounds.

July 24

Alison: What I learned here is to read * read to myself, try to make good—make it make sense.

Cathy: Make it make sense.

Alison: And pick Just Right and Vacation (Easy) books. ** Read more in class.

Cathy: Read more in class.

Alison: And teach myself how to, um um like, I can um read on and try to make it make sense to me.

Cathy: Good job, Alison. I think you're really in pretty good shape. I think you're in a position to teach yourself to read. As long as you know how to pick the right kind of book, and you read on, and you make it make sense, you're just gonna learn more and more words all the time.

guided her reflections on her successful problem solving. She again drew her attention to self-monitoring for meaning.

A few days later (July 16), Alison hesitated during her reading and then correctly identified the word *ducked*. When Cathy asked her to think back and explain her problem solving, Alison's responses indicated her growing awareness of monitoring her reading for meaning. Cathy reinforced her self-monitoring.

In their final reading conference (July 24), Cathy guided Alison's self-evaluations of her learning. In her reflections, Alison described her learning related to the general reading goals and clearly indicated her growing awareness of monitoring reading for meaning. Cathy's feedback verified Alison's self-assessments and clearly delineated what she needed to do to continue her reading progress.

These examples show that, over time, Cathy's explicit feedback and guided reflections fostered Alison's ability to self-monitor her reading for meaning. Alison's growing awareness and control of her reading processes were important steps on her path to reading independence.

Empowering Learners

When Susan and Marcia observed tutoring sessions, they found that explicit and clear instruction was vital to both novice teachers' and children's control of new learning. Susan observed Alice, a novice teacher, as she tutored a struggling reader, Jake. She describes the impact of explicit modeling on both Alice's and Jake's learning. Marcia observed Daniel, a child in the School Reading Partners Program (SRP). School Reading Partners are parent or community volunteers who provide beginning readers with extra practice and support. Daniel was observed in two different instructional settings—individual tutoring and the SRP classroom. She noticed that when Daniel gained control of his reading during his one-to-one tutoring sessions, he was empowered to become an "expert peer" capable of modeling and supporting strategic reading with other children in the SRP reading classroom. (See Figure 2.2 for a sample schedule of the SRP day.)

Alice and Jake

Alice wanted Jake to learn how to retell what he had read. After reading aloud a paragraph from a text, Jake was supposed to stop and tell what had happened in his own words and then think beyond the text to infer why it happened. Alice told Jake what she wanted him to do, but she did not model retelling processes for him. Consequently, when Jake finished reading a paragraph he did not use his own words to tell what he read and he made no effort to infer

Figure 2.2.
The School Reading Partners
Day

9:00–9:10	Opening
9:10–9:20	Read to Children
9:20–10:15	Reading Workshop
	Minilessons
	Conferences
	Independent Reading
	Partner Reading
	Reading Sharing
10:15–10:30	Recess
10:30–10:50	Read to Children
10:50–11:45	Project Workshop
	Minilessons
	Conferences
	Inquiry Projects
	Project Sharing
11:45–1:15	Lunch
1:15–2:00	One-on-One Tutoring
2:00–2:15	Recess
2:15–3:00	Small Group
	Day Care Reading
	Journal Writing
	Read to Children

causality. He simply repeated words from the text, and generally these were the last words he had read. For instance, he read the following text from *The Mummy Awakes* (Stine and Stine, 1993):

> *Text:* "Let's go," I said, pulling on Ben's arm. "Maybe it's the wind," Ben said. Certainly we heard the wind, it was Neshi. He's following me. And every second he came closer and I knew it.
>
> *Jake:* "It was Neshi and every second he came closer."

Alice did not intervene to model and explain the procedures she wanted Jake to follow and so he continued to repeat words from the text when retelling:

> *Text:* When I said that, Ben shook his head. He wouldn't believe in a living mummy, no matter how many footsteps he heard.
>
> *Jake:* He wouldn't believe in a living mummy.

Cathy Roller, Alice's university instructor, observed during Alice's and Jake's tutoring sessions. She realized that Alice did not understand how to help Jake learn to retell a story. She decided to model story retelling procedures both for Alice and for Jake, so in the next tutoring session Cathy taught Jake while Alice observed. Cathy began her instruction with the following explanation of what she expected Jake to do:

> *Cathy:* One of the things that's important when you're doing these retellings is that you tell me why things are happening, as well as what's happening. I like to know why it's happening.

After Jake read another paragraph from the text, he again simply repeated the last words he had read. He seemed confused when Cathy prompted his thinking:

> *Cathy:* Why does the author tell you that? What's the point he's trying to get across?
>
> *Jake:* I don't get what you're saying.
>
> *Cathy:* I'm trying to show you what I'd like you to do when I talk about explaining "why."

Realizing that she needed to make retelling procedures more explicit, Cathy next read a paragraph and then modeled retelling for Jake. She told what had happened and why she thought it happened. After modeling, she told Jake to try doing the same.

After Jake read another paragraph from *The Mummy Awakes*, Cathy scaffolded his learning. As Figure 2.3 shows, she gave him prompts that repeatedly focused his attention to the two critical concerns in retelling: what happened, and why did it happen?

After observing Cathy, Alice was able to use the same modeling techniques and consistent reminders when she worked with Jake. In their next tutoring session, she began by clearly stating expected retelling procedures:

> *Alice:* Read one paragraph at a time so you get a feel of what kinds of questions you want to ask. Not only . . . 'cause Dr. Roller told us on Friday, not only do we want to know what's happening, but why it's happening. Why characters say what they do.

She then modeled retelling procedures for Jake. First, she read a paragraph aloud. Then she retold what happened and explained why she thought it happened. Interestingly, Jake voluntarily joined in with his own thoughts about why the boys in *The Mummy Awakes* were so excited (in the transcript below, each asterisk indicates a pause of one second):

> *Text:* I unlocked the door and Carlos, Adam, and Ben were standing there. "Party!" The three of them chanted, pushing their way past me and dropping their sleeping bags in the living room.
>
> *Alice:* The boys came in and it sounds like they're just gonna start the party then.
>
> *Jake:* Well, I think maybe that uhh * * well, I thought this when you were reading. I thought it might have been Neshi making them say that?
>
> *Alice:* Yeah. Maybe.

Figure 2.3.
Modeling Retelling in
One-on-One Interaction

Dialogue Key

asterisk *	pause of one second per asterisk
bold type	child's self-correction
[brackets]	actual text words
ellipsis . . .	interruption
italics	child's reading of text
(parentheses)	added explanation
plain type	conversation
underlining	overlapping speech

Jake Learns Retelling

Text: We walked home in silence taking the long way, not through the park. When we got to Ben's I stayed there as long as I could, but finally I had to leave alone. I walked home looking over my shoulder the whole way.

Jake: When he got to Ben's house he stayed as long as he could.

Cathy: That's good. You said exactly what happened. Now tell me why. Why did he stay there as long as he could?

Jake: Because that way Neshi won't hurt him.

Cathy: So what I want you to do is to tell me what happened and why. It says here, "I walked home looking over my shoulder all the way." So what did he do?

Jake: He looked over his shoulder.

Cathy: And why?

Jake: That way he would know if someone is following him or not.

Cathy: So do you see what I mean? I want you to tell me what happened and why it happened. That was a very good example. Good job.

These examples illustrate that clear and explicit instruction was beneficial to both Jake's and Alice's learning.

Daniel

During individual tutoring sessions in SRP, Karen, Daniel's reading tutor, consistently promoted his understandings of reading strategies that would help him independently solve problems in text. When he needed her assistance she gave him clear prompts and cues to remind him of reading strategies he was learning. When picture cues could help him recognize a word, she asked, "What's happening in the picture? What are these?" When the context of a story could support his reading, she prompted him to skip a word and read on to search for clues to the word's meaning. She gave Daniel explicit feedback and guided his reflective thinking about his successful problem solving to promote his ability to monitor his reading for meaning.

Over time and with Karen's expert guidance, Daniel's repertoire of reading strategies grew. He began to self-monitor his reading for meaning and to automatically apply reading strategies to independently solve problems in text. In many instances he used picture cues along with sounds to help him decode unknown words, but at other times he would skip the word and read on to search for clues in the context. As illustrated in the following excerpt from a tutoring session, when Karen prompted Daniel's reflections on his successful reading, he could identify and explain his independent problem solving:

> *Karen:* I don't think . . . Did you get stuck on any words today?
>
> *Daniel:* Yeah, I think . . . I like said it wrong, but then I went back and . . .
>
> *Karen:* Why did you go back?
>
> *Daniel:* 'Cause it didn't sound right.
>
> *Karen:* It didn't sound right. That's great. That's a great strategy.

Moreover, when Daniel gained awareness and control in his own reading, he was empowered to support his classmates' reading. As the examples below illustrate, his interactions with his peers were remarkably similar to Karen's instructional actions.

Daniel could offer prompts and cues to scaffold reading for others. When he partner-read with Annie and Jeremy, he suggested alternative reading strategies to help them solve problems in text. For instance, when Jeremy came to the unknown word *filming,* he could articulate only the beginning sound. However, he persisted in sounding out the word and did not attempt other strategies. Daniel suggested that Jeremy look at the picture to see if it would help. Later on, he prompted both Jeremy and Annie to skip a word and read on when picture cues and sounds did not provide enough information to help them decode a word.

Daniel's expert role included explicit feedback and modeling. During another partner-reading session, his partner Craig struggled at first but then correctly identified the word *information* and then questioned his own problem solving. Craig looked at Daniel and said, "Information? I don't know. . . ." Daniel confirmed Craig's problem solving and reinforced his reading for meaning: "You're right. It makes sense that way."

As Craig and Daniel continued reading, they came to a difficult passage. Craig wanted to seek assistance from their teacher. Daniel responded, "I want to read the whole sentence first to see if I can get it." He then effectively modeled the skip-and-read-on strategy for Craig.

Daniel's interactions during partner reading with Richard also were highly consistent with Karen's supportive scaffolding during his tutoring. He offered Richard a series of prompts and cues to encourage problem solving, but he never let his partner struggle to the point of frustration. When Richard could not decode an unknown word, Daniel first encouraged independent problem solving. He prompted, "What can you do to figure this word out?" When Richard could not come up with any problem-solving strategies, Daniel suggested several. He pointed out specific picture cues that he thought might help and he gave hints about the word's meaning. When this strategy didn't work, he segmented the word, showing Richard the smaller word within the larger one. Recognizing that none of these strategies were working, he simply pronounced the word for Richard, and they continued reading.

These examples illustrate that Karen's clear instruction during tutoring sessions fostered Daniel's conscious awareness and control of his own reading processes and empowered him to become an expert who could influence learning in his peers.

Concluding Remarks

Our experiences with developing readers and novice teachers demonstrate that clear and explicit instruction is powerful. What we teach children and prospective teachers not only influences their own learning but also impacts learning in others.

We suggest, then, that clear instruction does not occur by happenstance but results from a set of instructional actions that teachers use consciously to promote learning. Expert teachers set appropriate learning goals that provide a framework for instruction and guide their instructional decisions. They scaffold learning with clear and explicit modeling and explanations. Their prompts and cues focus students' attention to critical aspects of the intended learning. They give students explicit feedback and guide their reflective thinking to foster a conscious awareness and control in learning. When responsible teachers recognize the power of their instructional actions, they ensure that what they say and do during instruction makes learning clear and accessible to their students.

Reference

Forsyth, S. A. (1997). *Individual reading conferences: Opportunities for learning from a sociocognitive perspective.* Unpublished doctoral dissertation, University of Iowa.

Children's Literature Cited

Randall, B. (1996). *Baby bear goes fishing*. New PM Storybooks. Crystal Lake, IL: Rigby.

Randall, B. (1996). *Baby bear's present*. New PM Storybooks. Crystal Lake, IL: Rigby.

Randall, B. (1996). *The hungry kitten*. New PM Storybooks. Crystal Lake, IL: Rigby.

Stine, M., & Stine, H. W. (1993). *The mummy awakes*. New York: Random.

Wood, A. (1992). *Silly Sally*. San Diego: Harcourt.

Driven to Read

Carrie Kawamoto

The author describes her work in supporting students as they build a repertoire of reading behaviors including slowing down, word pointing, and rereading, as she taught them to use different cueing systems. As she reflects on her reading program, Carrie looks closely at her practice to determine how to integrate changes based on her own readings on how children learn to read. She uses the "hypothesis-test" method (described in the introduction to Chapter 1), to learn alongside her student.

I am driven to read!!!! I am the *most* driven to read in this class!!!!" says Paul. "Me too!!!! I am driven too!!!" the others chime in. And Allison adds, "We are all driven!!!!"

Never—ever—in my more than 25 years of teaching have I ever seen children driven to read! The energy that flows from the joyful faces and bright eyes of these children is simply amazing.

Until two years ago, I thought I understood how to help my kindergartners learn to read and write. I immersed them in rich literature, songs, and print throughout the day. I worked at developing with parents, reinforcing how children learn, the values of reading aloud, and the stages of writing. I found ways to set up the learning environment so the children would be able to have time and choice to engage in real writing and real reading with real books. I worked at providing them with a safe environment so the children would take risks, learn from one another, and learn from their mistakes. But most important, I worked at building a positive relationship with each child. I based all my curricular decisions on what I understood about how children learn.

Then one day two years ago, a very significant thing happened in a graduate reading course taught by Dr. Diane Stephens. She told the class, "Teachers need to be able to tell parents, without the educational jargon, how children learn language—how children learn to talk, to write, and to read. We then need to be able to tell parents what curricular decisions we are making to help children with that learning." Her words jumped out at me because all those years, I had been basing my curricular decisions on what I understood about how children learn and applying the general principles

From *Primary Voices K–6*, 5(1), Jan. 1997, 24–34.

of learning to the teaching of reading. I don't ever recall thinking that I needed to understand the particulars of how children learn to read. I can't even remember anyone prompting me to *think* about how children learn to read. I was very surprised and very uncomfortable that I couldn't articulate how children learn to read. I did not have that knowledge base.

This disequilibrium propelled me to want to learn very specifically how children learn to read. But whom would I learn from? What distant voices could I listen to? As a part of that class, I became a part of an inquiry group that had this same driving inquiry. We decided to read and talk together about Frank Smith's *Understanding Reading* (1988) and *Reading without Nonsense* (1985), and David B. Doake's article on "Reading-Like Behavior: Its Role in Learning to Read" (1985). We also viewed home videos from Sally Burgett's (1992) and Tim O'Keefe's (1990) classrooms. I further studied Bobbi Fisher's *Joyful Learning* (1991), Carol Avery's . . . *And with a Light Touch* (1993), Marie Clay's *Reading Recovery* (1993) and *Observation Survey* (1993), Doake's *Reading Begins at Birth* (1988), and Constance Weaver's *Reading Process and Practice: From Socio-Psycholinguistics to Whole Language* (1994).

During this same time period, I was working one-on-one with one of my first graders, Tiffany. We met for one hour twice a week, as part of another graduate course I was taking with Diane Stephens. Diane had asked us to work with a child we wanted to help; I arranged to work with Tiffany instead. I didn't think Tiffany needed my help, but I needed hers. Tiffany paid close attention when I was reading stories to the class. During a conference at the beginning of the year, her dad said she was memorizing stories from books they had read to her. I expected that she would learn to read this year, and I wanted to see that process up close. I needed to understand how a child learned to read. I needed to make the connection from what I had been reading to the actual process as it played out for one child.

As I worked with Tiffany, I gathered my observational data and used the HT process to make sense of what I saw. It was, and continues to be, an amazing process. Working with one child gave me a new set of eyes, eyes that helped me really *see* Tiffany, and seeing her helped me see the other children in the classroom. The research that I was reading on how children learn to read came alive for me. In Figure 3.1, I have listed some of the hypotheses that I tested out with Tiffany that year in my effort to understand how children learn to read.

In September, when I read to Tiffany, she would echo me in certain parts of the text, read together with me the parts she knew, and listen quietly to other parts. In contrast to my former behavior of

Figure 3.1.
Some of the Hypotheses I
Tested While Working with
Tiffany

Could it be that if a child begins to make sense of environmental and book text, then it's likely that the child is aware that meaning is communicated through pictures and words?

Could it be, then, that the child would naturally want stories read, and want some stories read and reread?

Could it be that if the child was hearing familiar stories being reread, she would naturally engage in participatory reading?

Could it be that teachers and parents need to invite, not demand, that children engage in these participatory reading strategies in order to help in developing their reading-like behaviors?

Could it be that as the child "absorbs" the meaning of a story and begins to use his own language while "reading" a book, he is developing reading-like behaviors and very possibly developing his semantic and syntactic cueing systems?

Could it be that as the child begins constructing meaning by using her own language (syntactic cueing) to make meaning (semantic cueing), it then develops into the author's language, which the child "reads" with fluency and expression, often looking at the picture clues with very little attention to print while "reading"?

Could it be that the child sees reading-like behaviors as reading?

Could it be that parents may see these "reading-like behaviors" as rote memorization and view it as harmful and discourage their child from "reading" the same book over and over?

Could it be that many parents, believing that "sounding out" is the main strategy in learning to read, may unknowingly discourage naturally occurring reading-like behaviors by stressing only the "sounding-out" strategy?

Could it be that it is our job as teachers to educate parents on how children learn to read so parents will encourage participatory reading while reading aloud and come to value reading-like behaviors?

Could it be that we need to encourage a no-fail environment and a noncorrective environment as children develop their reading- like behaviors?

Could it be that as the child begins to watch the print while reading and tries to match the words to print, reading slowly, word for word, the child is developing his graphophonic cueing system?

Could it be that as the child begins to point to the word with her voice and/or fingers as she reproduces her favorite stories, she is focusing on the visual and phonic cueing system?

Could it be that the semantic and syntactic cueing systems appear to be ignored while the child focuses so intensely on the visual and phonic cueing system, but could actually already be in place, and so the child is able to give intense focus to the graphophonic cueing system?

Could it be that as the child overflows with a repertoire of reading-like behaviors from favorite stories, the child begins to read simple, unfamiliar texts word for word and grows to be a flexible reader, using all cueing systems while reading?

Could it be that a flexible strategic reader is one who sees reading as a problem-solving process and is able to figure out what strategy to use when he gets stuck in his reading?

Could it be that I need to look carefully as to what students do when they get stuck in their reading?

Could it be that I need to help them come to know the different strategies—rereading to make sense, looking at visual and phonic clues to make sense, substituting a word that makes sense, skipping and going on to make sense, using picture clues to make sense, predicting and confirming to make sense?

Could it be that I need to help value the strategies they already have?

Could it be that I need to think about the zone of proximal development in helping the children expand their knowledge and use of other strategies?

asking children to listen only, I encouraged Tiffany's participation. I did the same thing in the classroom. After rereading the same text a few times, I saw Tiffany and others move from using their own language to make meaning of the story to using the author's language. When I was reading *A Carrot Seed* (Krauss, 1945) to Tiffany for the second time, for example:

(Brackets indicate lines that we said simultaneously; italics means Tiffany read.)

Text	**Tiffany and Me**
a little boy planted a carrot seed.	a little [I pause] . . . *boy planted a carrot seed.*
His mother said, "I'm afraid it won't come up."	His [I pause] . . . *mother said it won't come up.*
His father said, "I'm afraid it won't come up."	His father said *it won't come up.*
And his big brother said, "It won't come up."	*And his big brother said it won't come up.*
Every day the little boy pulled the weeds around the seed and sprinkled the ground with water.	Every day [I pause] . . . *the little boy pulled weeds and watered the ground.*

During October, I could see close up Tiffany's driving force to expand her repertoire of reading-like behaviors. She would find others in the classroom to learn from. As she explained to me one day, "If you want to learn to read *Little Rabbit Foo Foo* (Rosen, 1993), you just go read with Justin because he knows it."

In November, I wondered if Tiffany would exhibit the "arrhythmical stage" that Doake talks about. And one day, very significantly, I saw her actually slow down while "reading" Resi Dietzel's *I Can Read* (1992). Tiffany read very confidently, very quickly, appearing not to be paying attention to print:

I can read about volcanoes.

I can read about surfing.

I can re—ad a—b—out . . .

Then her eyes looked very intently at the printed text and she slowed down, began to point at the words and reread it word for word, very slowly,

I . . . . can . . . . . read . . . . BOOKS . . . about . . . . skateboarding.

Tiffany was paying very close attention to the print to make sense of the story. She was even rereading, self-correcting all on her own. She was using all cueing systems to make sense of a text that previously she had just seemed to have "memorized." What a milestone! I shared what Tiffany did with the class so everyone could learn from what she did. I began to see more children reread, self-correct, and move on.

I wondered if Tiffany's repertoire of reading-like behaviors would overflow into reading simple, unfamiliar, predictable texts. When would she be able to use all cueing systems flexibly? Lo and behold, at our December session, I had shared a new predictable text *I Love You Goodnight* (Buller, 1988). Tiffany very flexibly used all three cueing systems as she made sense of this new predictable text. She used her prior knowledge to make sense of the text. When she came to unknown words, she looked at picture clues and initial letter of words (visual and phonic clues), she substituted words that made sense, and she did lots of rereading and self-correcting to make sense of the text. I was elated. I continued to see Tiffany move in and out of using two cueing systems, semantic and syntactic, and sometimes orchestrating all three cueing systems—semantic, syntactic, and graphophonemic—while reading predictable books.

At our December session, Tiffany also chose to read *Hop on Pop* (1963). She read it beautifully, using all cueing systems, and I asked her how she came to know this story so well. She had tried to read it in earlier sessions but struggled with it so she would ask me to read it while she engaged in the different participatory strategies. She echoed me, she read together with me, and sometimes just listened. She picked it up and asked others in class who knew the story to read it to her. Tiffany explained that she took the book home to have dad read it to her and she practiced reading it after listening and echoing with dad. She practiced reading it before dinner, after dinner, and before bed. She said she practiced at home many times. I began to find her reading it in class by herself or with others, helping herself and others to know *Hop on Pop*. What I saw her do, I began to see other children in class do when they wanted to learn a particular book. They listened to their friends/parents read to them, they echoed their friends/parents as they read, they read together parts they knew. It was so empowering!

Tiffany's reading just took off like a rocket ship into space. In February, she took home Shel Silverstein's *A Light in the Attic* (1981) and *Where the Sidewalk Ends* (1974). The next day, I saw her reading to her friends the poems that I had read in class. Others began to do the same. One mother even came to see me in the morning to tell me that she was shocked that her child was able to read some of Shel Silverstein's poems.

In late February and March, after Tiffany listened to me read *Abiyoyo* (Seeger, 1988), *Wednesday's Surprise* (Bunting, 1988), *Salamander Room* (Mazer, 1991), and many other nonpredictable books, she picked them up and read them by herself or with friends. She also took them home to practice and was able to read them using different reading strategies to help her make sense of the text.

In the final months of school, April, May, and June, Tiffany found books in the classroom library that she wanted to learn to read—books that I had not yet read to the class but encouraged them to read. She continued to find ways to teach herself to read the books, especially Arnold Lobel's Frog and Toad series (e.g., *Frog and Toad Are Friends,* 1973).

Because of what I learned from Tiffany, I continually watched to see what individual children did when they came to unknown words, and helped them reflect on the strategies they used or could use when they get stuck. I wanted to help them see that reading is a problem-solving process and that they needed to figure out which strategies would be most helpful in a particular situation. By sharing what I discovered with the rest of the class, I found others able to do the same. They were learning from each other.

For example, one morning, I saw Allison reading *Green Eggs and Ham* (1960). I listened very carefully and noticed she was using semantics, syntax, and graphophonemic cueing systems as she read. Tiffany quickly got another copy of *Green Eggs and Ham* and began echoing Allison. I asked Allison, "How do you know how to read *Green Eggs and Ham?*" She replied, "I watched the video a lot. So now I want to learn how to read *Green Eggs and Ham.*" She was connecting what she knew in her head to the printed text. Many mornings and during workshop time, I found Allison glued to the book, sometimes with Tiffany. She took the book home every night until her mom got her own copy. That morning, after I shared Allison's strategy of making connections between what she had seen and what she read, Justin and Calvin began to read *Green Eggs and Ham* together, unsuccessfully trying to hide the two copies so no one else could get to them at the next reading time. "Can you buy more *Green Eggs and Ham*?" Calvin asked. "We want to read *Green Eggs and Ham* but there aren't enough books." I asked the class, "How many of you have *Green Eggs and Ham* at home? Could you bring them to school?" Paul, Ikaika, and Kelii brought theirs from home. Joyce went to the store to buy her own copy. Bob went to the library to get his copy. *Green Eggs and Ham* began to spread like wildfire!!

Justin took *Green Eggs and Ham* home many times. His daily reading log showed that each time he borrowed it, he read with his mom or big sister more than once each evening, sometimes three or four times. He logged in readings on Saturdays and Sundays as well.

In the morning, during settling-in periods, I saw him reading by himself or asking others to read with him. They could read it well. One morning, he shared with me, "Last night, my two-year-old cousin Jon was crying and my Grandma told Jon to go to bed or she was going to spank him. I told Grandma, don't spank Jon. I'm going to read him *Green Eggs and Ham*. When I was finished reading the book, Jon was sleeping." What a precious story!

For several weeks, Justin was reading *Green Eggs and Ham*. He would practice and practice, sometimes reading it with Chris, Paul, and others. Soon these others began to follow Justin's lead. They found friends to read with during the settling-in periods, during transitional periods throughout the day, and during reading workshop time. They would choose to read it together with their Title I teacher. They would take it home to read with their parents, practicing the story many, many times with others and by themselves, using the different participatory strategies. They also knew the different strategies to use when they got stuck in their reading. They knew that picture clues in the book were extremely helpful. They also understood that rereading and self-correcting helped them to make sense of their reading. They would sometimes substitute a word that they thought would make sense. They used visual and phonetic clues to make sense of their reading.

Whenever I saw a child exhibiting a reading strategy, I would share it with the rest of the class. But reading together, helping one another, was the powerful ingredient in learning to read *Green Eggs and Ham*. They echoed or repeated the story with one another, they read together parts they knew, and still there were others who "mumbled" along with their partners. The children were learning to use reading strategies to read with partners in school or at home with their parents or siblings. Bringing the books home every night to practice was also another critical factor in helping them learn to love to read.

Each week, I introduced more books to the class. I gave book talks and read to the children every day, some books more than once. Just as individual students had done, the children read parts they knew together with me, and just listened in other parts. Each book I read was an invitation—an invitation to the children to pick it up and learn to read by reading it with a friend, their parents, or older siblings at home. That year, children brought home 2–4 books every night. Reading together with partners is powerful stuff.

As I listened to the children read that year, I could clearly see that they had come to know that reading is making meaning, and that it is a problem-solving process of figuring out what to do when one gets stuck. So many of the children drove themselves to learn to read, and they positively affected many of their siblings. Parents told me about younger siblings who were beginning to exhibit reading-like behaviors, and older siblings came to borrow books from our classroom library.

Working one-on-one with Tiffany that year taught me that to be truly helpful to children as readers, I needed to see what was happening as the children were reading with partners and alone. And I needed to bring what I was seeing to the rest of the class so we could learn from each other.

The HT process provided the framework that helped me do this. In order to see, however, I needed a knowledge base about how children learn to read. I developed that knowledge base by watching how Tiffany taught herself to read, and by reading and rereading professional books and articles. The learning cycle never stops.

Lingering Questions

1. Five of my students did echo reading with children who knew *Green Eggs and Ham*, but only occasionally. They knew parts of the story. But I wonder why they did not choose to learn the entire book. Why were they not as driven as the rest of the class? My lingering questions are possible Interpretations:

- Could it be that the text was too long?
- Could it be that the text was too difficult and they needed simpler texts?
- Could it be they were simply not interested in learning *Green Eggs and Ham?*
- Could it be they need to know more explicitly how we can come to learn to read books?
- Could it be they need to hear this story many more times, by echo reading with friends or parents?
- Could it be they need to want to take it home to practice with their parents and themselves?
- Could it be they may have more important things on their minds and find it difficult to drive themselves to want to learn the story?
- Could it be they need daily one-on-one teacher instruction to make real progress? But how could this be done within the school day? Could using predictable books, written especially for beginning readers (e.g., Wright Story Box books) help these children?

2. How do I organize and make sense of my daily Observations so that I can make Interpretations, Hypotheses, and Curricular Decisions to help my children as readers and writers?

3. How do I organize my data for children, parents, and the larger community? How do I integrate the data into the quarterly report card?

Classroom Connections by Carrie Kawamoto			
If the child...	makes up stories to go with picture books reads the print in the environment (print in room, in school, on street, in stores) rereads familiar, predictable books	begins to exhibit a more arrhythmical quality in his or her reading-like behavior reproduces stories more deliberately, more methodically begins to watch the print while reading, trying to match the words to print, reading slowly, word for word begins to point to the word with voice and/or fingers while reproducing favorite stories focuses on visual cueing system, paying intense attention to print while reading begins to use beginning consonant to help read unfamiliar words begins to develop strategies to help unlock unfamiliar words (self-corrects)	begins to read simple unfamiliar texts word for word fluently reads familiar texts uses all cueing systems asks him- or herself, "Does it make sense?" "Does it sound right?" "Can we say it that way?" "Does it look right?" wants to read to adults
It could mean that...	the child is aware that meaning can be communicated through pictures and words	semantic and syntactic cueing could be already in place, but the child appears to be ignoring them in order to focus attention on graphophonemic cueing system directionality is becoming established concepts of a "word" and a "letter" are emerging the child realizes that print on the pages plays an important role in the reading process	the child is aware when something doesn't make sense, doesn't sound right, doesn't look right the child is on the way to becoming a strategic reader
Once you were "pretty sure" this was true, you could...	provide a variety of reading materials for children to choose from: environmental print provide lots of time throughout the day for children to read together . . . by themselves, with a friend or friends, with the teacher, with the whole class provide Daily Read-Alouds, at least 2–3 times a day with varied literature of fiction and nonfiction encourage children to make personal connections ask, "What are you thinking?" provide time for children to write by writing encourage experimentation and approximation by having them choose what they want to write about provide a message board for children to communicate with the class and with one another provide time for children to go to different centers where they can make sense of things with writing tools and text . . . home living, music center, blocks, writing center, easel painting, clay provide writing tools at writing center: water colors, crayons, pens, scissors, glue, stapler, different kinds of paper provide daily Shared Reading Time introduce new song, poem, or chant for the week print out text for class Big Book print out individual song books that will be taken home weekly	have children ask themselves, "Does it make sense?" "Does it sound right?" "Does it look right?" encourage reading strategies: ■ Making predictions ■ Confirming predictions ■ Skipping and going on ■ Using prior knowledge ■ Rereading ■ Asking someone ■ Substituting ■ Using visual and phonic clues	continue all previous strategies, remembering at all times that the most disempowered people are those who cannot read and who turn away from books and print in frustration those are also disempowered who can read but choose not to do so literacy can help people develop an inner sense of power to control their own learning and direct their own lives to grow and feel confident

Resource Box 2

Resource Box 3

Connecting with Parents by Carrie Kawamoto

It is important that parents understand our goals and expectations early on in the school year. We want them to become our partners, and to participate in reading with their children.

At the Open House at the beginning of the year, I make a point to explain the value of reading aloud and I tell the parents that their children will be bringing home each night one Read-Aloud Book that the parent can read to the child and one predictable book that the child can read to the parent. I also ask parents to find ways to get other books to their children.

These occasions when parents are together as a group are ideal times to stress the crucial importance of children's home experience with books. Here are some of the areas I explain:

- why, how, and what parents could be reading to children.
- how children learn to read.
- what I do to help children learn to read: invite, not demand child's participation in reading; help child to become aware of participatory strategies; help child to see reading as making sense, not decoding and answering comprehension questions.
- that seeing reading as mainly decoding can cause problems in the reading process for children.

Early in the first quarter, students take home a packet containing a letter to parents that explains how children learn to read, asks parents and children to record what the child reads, and asks parents to write notes to the teacher about the children's reading (see packet samples that follow). Throughout the rest of the year, I continue to work with parents, helping them to understand their role in the reading development of their children, by developing parent involvement activities, workshops, and newsletters; and encouraging a dialogue journal between home and school.

Dear Parents,

I am asking for your help in the *reading development of your kindergartner* because I have come to know that with the family's help, your child can learn so-o much more!!!

I will be helping every kindergartner to learn to love books because being able to read will help them to do well in school and to feel good about themselves, and the stories we read can help us to make sense of our lives and to lead more meaningful lives.

Every night, all of the kindergartners will bring home two books, which they will choose from the classroom library. One of them is a Read-Aloud book, which a family member (Mom, Dad, Grandma, Grandpa, Big Brother, Big Sister) may read to your kindergartner as he or she listens. The other is a "predictable book," which your kindergartner will "read" to you. Oftentimes they will be bringing home familiar books, which we have already read in class. I am encouraging them to return to their favorite books.

Your child will probably begin "reading" by using his or her own words while "reading" the story from what he or she remembers of the text and from all that he or she knows about the world and by using the picture clues, *not* the printed text. Each time your child returns to a favorite book, the "reading" will develop into what appears to be memorization of the story. **In this critical learning to read process, I ask that you encourage your child to "read" in a noncorrective, no-fail environment, so he or she will not turn away from the books.**

Amazingly, the books will teach your child to read. Each time your child returns to the familiar books, something "magic" happens within the brain. As your child comes to know many, many stories, your child will begin to connect the "memorized" stories in his head to the printed text in the book. This is all part of the process of learning to read. As the year progresses, your child may want to borrow more than two books.

continued on next page

**Resource Box 3
continued**

Last school year, one of my parents wrote and said, "I never knew how much a young child could learn . . . so fast. I thought teaching my children how to read was very hard, but it just takes lots of patience and lots of reading together as a family . . . ." Dear Parents—when we work together, we can do so much for our kindergartners.

Thank you very much,
Carrie Kawamoto

Dear Parents,

Would you please take some time out of your very busy schedule (once a week perhaps) to write comments or questions about what's happening during your Reading Time at home? I would like to share some of the comments with the class so that we may learn from one another. If you wish confidentiality on the comments, please indicate so.

Thank you very much,
Carrie Kawamoto

- -

Comments by Parents and/or Child

Reading Log

Date	Title of Book	Person Who Read Book
1.		
2.		
3.		
4.		
5.		
6.		
7.		
8.		
9.		
10.		

Reflection Point

Breaking the code of language is one of the families of practices described by Luke and Freebody (1999) that are essential for literacy learning. Each of the teachers in the three articles worked with their students on decoding various fundamental features of language. For instance, in the first article Dianne Yoshizawa worked with Jaime to decode letters and words in order to support him as a beginning writer. In the third article Carrie Kawamoto helped her student Tiffany to use different cueing systems as she learned to read. This is the kind of code-breaking practice we are most aware of. We are less aware of the cultural models that undergird why we do what we do and why students react to our teaching in particular ways.

Think about Daniel, for instance, one of the students in the SRP program written about in the second article. When his teacher noticed he had "gained control of his reading," he was "empowered to become an expert peer." Once he was given this designation he was positioned differently in the classroom. For instance, when Daniel and his classmate Craig came across a difficult passage while reading together, Craig wanted to seek assistance from their teacher. Daniel responded, "I want to read the whole sentence first to see if I can get it." He then modeled the skip-and-read-on strategy for Craig.

The cultural models we bring to a situation make a difference in the kinds of social practices with which we engage. Clearly Craig and Daniel brought different cultural models to the reading of the difficult passage. The cultural model Craig operated from was, "If I have problems all I have to do is ask my teacher." Daniel brought a totally different cultural model to the learning situation, namely, "I'm the expert peer so I can solve this problem."

How might our teaching practices influence the kinds of cultural models our students bring to a learning situation?

Use the chart to think about the kinds of common code-breaking practices you engage in with your students and the various cultural models that come into play in your curricular decision making.

Code Breaking and Cultural Models

Common code-breaking practices I use in my classroom	Cultural models that come into play in my curricular decision making

References   Avery, C. (1993). *. . . . And with a light touch*. Portsmouth, NH: Heinemann.

Buller, J. (1988). *I love you goodnight*. New York: Simon.

Bunting, E. (1988). *Wednesday's surprise*. New York: Trumpet.

Burgett, S. (1992). Unpublished classroom video.

Clay, M. (1993). *Observation survey*. Portsmouth, NH: Heinemann.

Clay, M. (1993). *Reading recovery*. Portsmouth, NH: Heinemann.

Dietzel, R. (1992). *I can read*. Honolulu: Bess Press.

Doake, D. (1985). Reading-like behavior: Its role in learning to read. In A. Jaggar & T. Smith-Burke (Eds.), *Observing the language learner* (pp. 82–98). Urbana, IL: NCTE.

Doake, D. (1988). *Reading begins at birth*. Canada: Scholastic.

Fisher, B. (1991). *Joyful learning*. Portsmouth, NH: Heinemann.

Krauss, R. (1945). *A carrot seed*. New York: Harper.

Lobel, A. (1970). *Frog and Toad are friends*. New York: Harper.

Luke, A., and Freebody, P. (1999). Further notes on the four resources model. *Practically Primary, 1,* 99.

Mazer, A. (1991). *Salamander room*. New York: Trumpet.

O'Keefe, T. (1990). Unpublished classroom video.

Rosen, M. (1993). *Little rabbit Foo Foo*. New York: Simon.

Seeger, P. (1988). *Abiyoyo*. New York: Simon.

Seuss, Dr. (1960). *Green eggs and ham*. New York: Random.

Seuss, Dr. (1963). *Hop on Pop*. New York: Random.

Silverstein, S. (1974). *Where the sidewalk ends*. New York: Harper.

Silverstein, S. (1981). *A light in the attic*. New York: Harper.

Smith, F. (1985). *Reading without nonsense*. New York: Teachers College Press.

Smith, F. (1988). *Understanding reading*. Mahwah, NJ: Erlbaum.

Weaver, C. (1994). *Reading process and practice: From socio-psycholinguistics to whole language*. Portsmouth, NH: Heinemann.

II Practices That Support Meaning Making

How we conceptualize literacy makes a difference, because our conceptualizations underpin both the practices we engage in ourselves and those we create for our students. In our best imagination of the future, multiple literacies will be used to generate multiple perspectives, and the diversity of multiple perspectives will be used to generate tension and propel learning. "Multiple literacies" refers to the different ways that we construct and negotiate meaning in the world, e.g., print literacy, media literacy, or technological literacy. Further, given a student population that is increasingly diverse linguistically and culturally, our conceptualization should make use of that diversity in our classrooms to explore what different teaching practices make a difference in the lives of our students and what difference these differences make.

In this section of the book we have selected stories of practice that illustrate teachers working through issues of diversity and multiple literacies. Luke and Freebody ("A Map of Possible Practices: Further Notes on the Four Resources Model," *Practically Primary*, 4(2), 1999, pp. 5–8), who, along with other educators, argue for an ever-evolving set of literacy practices in school that reflect the social construction of literacy in communities at large, describe such practices this way:

> Effective literacy draws on a repertoire of practices that allow learners [. . .] to participate in understanding and composing meaningful written, visual and spoken texts, taking into account each text's interior meaning systems in relation to their available knowledge and their experience of other cultural discourses, texts, and meaning systems. (1999, p. 5)

We take this to mean that learners bring to their schooling a particular repertoire of experiences and that those experiences should be engaged and expanded for literacy learning to be most effective. For instance, in the first article included in this section, Amy Wackerly and Beth Young make use of the repertoire of literacy skills brought to school by second grader Gregory as a way of making the curriculum accessible to him. Making curriculum accessible includes putting to use a diverse range of meaning systems, including those that learners bring from their communities, families, cultures, and institutions.

The articles included in this section are "Community, Choice, and Content in the Urban Classroom," by A. Wackerly and B. Young, "Revising Teaching: Drawing, Writing, and Learning with My Students," by E. Olbrych, and "Units of Study in the Writing Workshop," by I. T. Nia.

Reflection Point

As you read through the articles in this section, note instances of teachers' valuing and extending the mean-making processes the students bring to their learning. Reflect on the following questions:

How did practices outside the school matter within it?
What meaning-making processes came into play?
How did the classroom teacher address issues of diversity?
In what ways were multiple literacies used in the classroom?

Community, Choice, and Content in the Urban Classroom

Amy Wackerly and Beth Young

The authors together teach a combined second- and third-grade class. They characterize their school as a place that listens to what kids have to say and then provides them with opportunities to explore their compelling questions in multiple ways. Gregory, a student who would stand a good chance of being labeled "at risk" in other school settings, is able to engage his interest in snakes through browsing books and the Internet, conducting interviews, taking notes, writing up his findings, and presenting his new knowledge to the classroom community. It is the community that supports and sustains his efforts as he develops skills for participating in this meaning-focused curriculum.

As Gregory enters Mrs. Young's 2–3 class, he chooses to settle in with a magazine and the class turtle, Boxer. His choice was made from several options because choice is at the very heart of classrooms at the Center for Inquiry (CFI). Gregory could have chosen to begin the day by reading independently or with a friend. He could have decided to work on the Knowledge Board, which presents a wide variety of problems to solve, from using the world map to find the northernmost continent to using the daily newspaper to find articles on the celebration of Dr. King's birthday. But this morning, Gregory chose the company of Boxer and the slower pace of browsing a magazine. We'll peek in on Gregory throughout the day to keep an eye on the role choice plays in the learning lives of children in these classrooms.

The idea of choice in the classroom, though central to our teaching, is not a new one. In fact, educators have been writing about and discussing this topic for decades. However, with the push for high-stakes testing, state and district mandates, and programs over people, it's a challenge for educators to find ways to give students choices and to let those choices drive the curriculum.

From *Primary Voices K–6, 10*(3), Jan. 2002, 17–23.

Alfie Kohn (1993), a proponent of choice, argues in favor of classrooms without extrinsic motivation or the many control factors often forced upon students. Instead, he advocates the three Cs of motivation: content, community, and choice. Kohn explains that students must find the content interesting, relevant, and somehow worth knowing (as quoted in Brandt, 1995). He contends that students need to know they are in a safe and caring environment—that is, in a community where they do not feel manipulated or coerced into sharing, doing their work, or participating in class. According to Kohn, students are able to enjoy the social aspect of learning through cooperation and collaboration when in a community of learners. And finally, Kohn states, ". . . the irrefutable fact is that students always have a choice about whether they will learn. We may be able to force them to complete an assignment, but we can't compel them to learn effectively or to care about what they are doing" (Kohn, 1993, p.12).

Through choice, making decisions that help guide their education, students are able to take ownership of their learning. From our experiences, we know that when children are "into" what they're learning, they are more vested. To give the students more ownership of their education, we involve them in decision making the moment they walk into the classroom, giving them a voice and allowing them to take control of their learning. Choice is the key characteristic of an environment where inquiry can thrive. Choice is our foundation.

As the day progresses, we see Gregory and his classmates moving into a class meeting, a regular morning ritual. Students greet each other in a variety of ways and Colleen reads the agenda for the day from the board. Gregory settles in next to his buddy Sam and anxiously waits his turn to share. It is difficult for him to listen to others, but the speaker waits, with a pointed look at Gregory, for the group's attention. Later, math time brings the opportunity to work with a partner. Problems are solved in many ways, and all solutions are valued and discussed. Today, partners are assigned by Mrs. Young and Gregory moves off to work with Raven. They are working on regrouping and Raven, who is more advanced in math than Gregory, sees that he is struggling and sends him off to get some Unifix cubes. They complete their work together, with Gregory more confident in regrouping and Raven strengthening her skills as the "teacher."

Next on the day's agenda is journaling time. During daily journal writing, students are allowed to write about anything they choose. Ideas vary from written conversation with a friend, to chapter books, to poetry, to nonfiction pieces, to fiction, to real-life stories. Gregory chooses to write about his new cat, and he quickly gets to work. After editing, he decides to move the story to his author's folder so that he can take the piece to publication. At lunch, students choose where they will sit, and Gregory moves to the table where his older sister waits. They talk animatedly, sharing the happenings of the morning. As they move outside for recess, they run off to play with their separate friends.

After lunch and recess, a large block of the afternoon is devoted to literature study. As students settle in around the room to read the books of their choice, Gregory pulls a pillow into the coat closet and proudly shows Mrs. Young the chapter book he is reading. This book is quite challenging for him, but his desire is strong. He struggles with a few words, but with some help, he uses various strategies to figure them out, and he makes it through the chapter. Mrs. Young asks him some questions about what happened in this part of the book and he struggles to retell the story, often looking back at the text. She asks him why he chose this book, and he hesitates. "Because it's a chapter book," he says. Many of his peers are reading chapter books and this has been a goal for Gregory. Mrs. Young asks Gregory to recall how to choose a book that is just right for him. He tells her, "It should have a few words I don't know, but not too many." She asks if he thinks this book has just a few words he doesn't know, and he admits that there are many. As they talk, Gregory agrees to keep this book as a read-aloud for home and to choose another book, with Mrs. Young's help, to work on for his independent reading.

The afternoon ends with time for inquiry. The class is studying Indianapolis because the school recently moved from the northeast side of the city to the downtown area. Gregory browses among the invitations (Short & Harste, 1996) that are set out around the classroom. There are several open-ended projects that focus on our city. One asks students to use the magazines, maps, brochures, and guidebooks to plan their perfect day in Indianapolis with unlimited funds! Another invitation shows the students the artwork of two Hoosier artists, T. C. Steele and Robert Indiana, and asks them to notice their very different styles. The students then attempt to create a painting imitating the style of one of the artists. Gregory finally chooses to work on an invitation that asks the students to create a sign welcoming visitors to our city and begins to draw. At the end of the time, he records some new information in his log and shares his sign with the students at his table.

This day full of choices ends—predictability without programs, perimeters without boundaries. Each day follows a similar schedule, and the agenda is posted every morning; students know what to expect. But the day is not set in stone; there is flexibility. Students are given guidelines and ideas, but they are also free to take ideas and choices as far as they can. At CFI, we do this without teacher's manuals that dictate our teaching, but we do follow the curriculum framework for our school district. Everything that is necessary is "covered," but students are given various levels of choice within these guidelines.

Content: The Glue That Holds It All Together

Although we view choice as the foundation and the key characteristic of an environment where inquiry can thrive, like Kohn, we recognize the essential role of content in the learning lives of our students. Indianapolis Public Schools are no different from schools in other school districts, so at CFI, we are required to work within a mandated curricular framework. Even so, both the teachers and students have room to make choices. The Center for Inquiry implies by its very name that inquiry is present in all the classrooms. In an inquiry classroom, students are involved in choosing what they learn and how they learn it.

Since we agree with Kohn that content must be interesting, relevant, and somehow worth knowing, we make sure that the opportunity for choice is available as we make decisions about the broad topics for inquiry studies. Often the topics for our large, whole-class inquiry studies are based on district and state requirements. For example, second and third graders are required to study animals, their life cycles and habitats. Other times, events in the world around us help us to choose topics. Our Indianapolis study was a natural choice as we moved downtown to our new neighborhood. A few years ago, we did a study of the Grand Canyon because a parent was hiking to the bottom and offered to set up a Web site so that we could follow his adventures.

Children are involved in these decisions as well. For example, during the past school year, the focus of one large inquiry study was animals. We began by creating a KWL chart to find out what the students already knew about animals and what they wanted to find out. We do this to guide our planning and to increase the possibility that the content will be interesting and worth knowing. As we expected, students' interests varied widely, so we asked each student to choose one animal to study in depth.

Gregory chose snakes. Various open-ended invitations were set up to help students discover facts and information about their particular animal. Through the invitations he selected, Gregory read and researched a variety of topics including habitat, diet, reproduction, types of snakes, and unusual facts about many kinds of snakes. As a struggling reader, Gregory often found this work challenging, but his interest level was high because he was allowed some choice in content. His personal investment in the subject matter kept him going even though he needed a great deal of support. Gregory and his classmates were working well within the curricular framework set forth by our district while making choices about the specific topics of their personal inquiry as well as decisions about the partners with whom they worked.

Students are encouraged to work on independent inquiry topics of their choice, and our curriculum often takes off on student-led tangents. These inquiries vary from a fan finding out details of Britney Spears's life to a student wanting to investigate a praying mantis he saw to a study of the gall bladder because of a sister's recent operation. Students spend time both at school and at home reading and researching their topics of interest and creating ways to present what they have learned to the class. A roomful of students learns about each topic because of one person's interest. What a way to broaden the curriculum!

As the animal study came to a close, Gregory informed us that he wanted to continue studying snakes. This was the first time he had expressed an interest in doing an independent inquiry project. Clearly he had found content that was engaging and worth knowing. Off he went to the library to collect more information. After some browsing, he concluded that he wanted to find out more about the largest snakes. This narrowing of his topic became a great focusing question for his inquiry. Each day, he used a chunk of classroom time to read and research on the Internet. He had difficulty focusing on important information and wanted to write down everything he saw. We paired him up with Joshua, a student who could help him weed out unimportant information and take notes on only the details he needed.

Another struggle, for Gregory and others, was putting information into his own words. Some older students who regularly help in the classroom assisted him with putting his information in "kid language." After several weeks, Gregory was ready to read his report and answer questions. For Gregory, it was a defining moment in the classroom. He was on his own in front of his peers, sharing his knowledge of snakes. Students asked questions and gave him feedback. They told him of some areas where he needed improvement (a louder speaking voice, more details, a larger picture) but they also gave him great encouragement. For the first time, he was the expert. He beamed with pride and was ready to begin another independent inquiry project.

Community: A Building Block for Inquiry

The choices that Gregory and his classmates make each day assume a sense of trust. There is a trust that teachers will support and guide you. There is a trust that classmates will come to your aid when you struggle. There is a trust that if your decisions prove to be less than wise, your community will be there for you. Choice in the classroom means risk taking. When students are allowed to choose what they want to learn, they have to step out on a limb. They don't have an entire class doing the exact same thing to back them up. They must, as Kohn reminds us, feel safe and cared for. They must feel supported, not coerced or manipulated. They must know they are members of a caring community of co-learners.

At CFI, community is something that begins in the classroom and extends throughout the building and into the larger community. One thing we feel sets us apart is the amount of input that students have in decision making. Having a voice in the classroom and the school as a whole empowers students and gives them a feeling of ownership and belonging. (See "Ways to Build Community," Figure 4.1.) This voice builds common bonds and strengthens personal connections that are essential to a sense of community.

Community is vital in an inquiry-based classroom because learning is social. As teachers share their passions and ideas, students begin to feel comfortable doing the same. Students come to know their teacher and one another in ways that may be lacking in more traditional settings. This level of trust and mutual understanding leads to developing the skills necessary for working with a partner or small group on inquiry projects. Developing those human connections, shared interests, and mutual respect is one important way of building expertise in the community. That expertise becomes yet another resource for both group and individual inquiry. "Experts" may come in the form of a kindergarten student who knows a lot about dinosaurs or an adult who has hiked the Grand Canyon and can give input on animal life in the West.

For Gregory, community means support. You may remember that we began our day with a class meeting. This morning, Gregory was welcomed into the circle with a handshake and a greeting. He is an important member of this class, and we are interested in his life. When he shared the news that he will be visiting his cousin this weekend, he was bombarded with questions.

Later during math, when Gregory struggled to focus and work with his group, Breana used an "I" message to let him know, in a positive way, that his behavior was keeping them from completing their work. When this didn't work, a time-out was needed, and Gregory moved to another part of the room to work on his own. It didn't take long for him to realize that he needed and wanted to be back in the community of his peers. A brief talk helped him to see what changes needed to be made for him to join his group, and he was off to try again within the folds of his community.

At lunchtime, choosing lunch partners and chatting with other students of various ages extends that community beyond the classroom. After lunch, when Gregory worked on his inquiry project

Figure 4.1.
Ways to Build Community in
the Inquiry-Based Classroom

- Class meetings to greet and share with our classroom community
- Town meetings to address problems and concerns
- Schoolwide community meetings to share and celebrate learning
- Focused discovery clubs for students of all ages to learn about topics of interest to them
- Student Council to give students a voice in school issues
- Parent Teacher Student Association (PTSA) to encourage students to be involved in all areas of school decision making
- Peer mediation to train students to help others solve problems in a peaceful way
- Social action projects to allow students to be involved in the community and the world around them

about snakes, he took the opportunity to talk with Mr. Turner, a 4–5 teacher who has a snake in his classroom and is an "expert."

Throughout this day, and every other day, that sense of community supports, guides, and teaches the students in the classrooms at CFI. And because of that support, along with the opportunity to make choices that impact the relevance of the content to be studied, Gregory and his classmates can be risk-takers, learners.

What about Standards and Accountability?

An inquiry-based curriculum full of choice, content that is personally relevant, a supportive classroom, and school-wide community—it does sound wonderful. Interested, motivated students, hardworking dedicated teachers, lots of excitement—that sounds wonderful, too. But what about tests? What about reports to parents? What about accountability?

Indianapolis Public Schools operate with the same requirements as any other school district across the nation. There are mandates, there are tests, and there are expectations . . . high expectations. And why shouldn't there be? It is the largest school district in the state of Indiana, located in the center of the state capital and within walking distance of some of the world's leading educational research and learning facilities. As in schools everywhere, students often come to us with various problems and concerns, but expectations are high, as they must be, no matter what the barriers. We feel that our urban students should be held to the same high expectations as the students in the suburban schools. And we firmly believe they are capable of achieving those goals.

Assessment looks different when inquiry and choice drive the curriculum, but it is there. As Gregory and his classmates are working, we are continually "kid watching" and jotting down notes on a clipboard. Gregory's animal log, the artifacts he creates at invitations, his written report on snakes, and his self-assessments are filed into his portfolio. A literature study often ends with a paper/pencil "test," using some recall questions and some more open-ended questions. Each week, Gregory and other students are asked to complete a written language evaluation covering the basic skills we've been working on in class. Teachers record benchmarks to keep track of what skills have been covered and whether students have mastered those skills.

At the end of each nine-week grading period, teachers write a detailed narrative report for each student that accounts for everything that has gone on in the classroom in all areas of the curriculum. Teachers must also reflect on each part of the curriculum and list the child's strengths and challenges in each area along with specific goals to work toward in the next nine weeks. Students and parents are asked to add goals of their own. Teachers also meet with parents and students twice a year, at the end of the first and third grading periods, to look at the child's portfolio and discuss progress.

CFI is required to follow the same curricular guidelines and take the same standardized tests as the rest of our district. In Indiana, third-, sixth-, and eighth-grade students are required to take the ISTEP (Indiana Statewide Testing for Educational Progress) in September. Our district also requires grades 1–8 to take another test in March. Our students do well on these tests, near the top of our district. We feel they do well because we teach them to be learners. And because they are avid readers and writers and inquirers, they are developing a broad knowledge base.

Giving children the freedom to make choices has shown us as educators what children can do when given the opportunity in a supportive community with a relevant curriculum. Inquiry-based learning is built on choice. As Gregory and his classmates show us, involving our urban students in inquiry makes perfect sense. We accept all learners, and we value the experiences each of them brings to school. With choice as our foundation, and content and community as the building blocks, we create an interesting and successful urban school. As teachers loosen the reins of control and hand them over to students, amazing things can happen.

References   Brandt, R. (1995). Punished by rewards? A conversation with Alfie Kohn. *Educational Leadership, 53*(1), 13–16.

Kohn, A. (1993). Choices for children: Why and how to let children decide. *Phi Delta Kappan, 75,* 8–20.

Short, K. G., & Harste, J. (with Burke, C.). (1996). *Creating classrooms for authors and inquirers.* Portsmouth, NH: Heinemann.

Resource Box 4

Growing Your Knowledge Base

Charney, R. S. (1992). *Teaching children to care: Management in the responsive classroom.* Greenfield, MA: Northeast Foundation for Children.

Csikszentmihaliyi, M. (1990). *Flow: The psychology of optimal performance.* New York: Harper.

Harvey, S. (1998). *Nonfiction matters: Reading, writing, and research in grades 3–8.* York, ME: Stenhouse.

Hindley, J. (1996). *In the company of children.* York, ME: Stenhouse.

Ladson-Billings, G. (1994). *The dream keepers: Successful teachers of African-American children.* San Francisco: Jossey.

Peterson, R. (1992). *Life in a crowded place: Making a learning community.* Portsmouth, NH: Heinemann.

Routman, R. (1991). *Invitations.* Portsmouth, NH: Heinemann.

Routman, R. (2000). *Conversations.* Portsmouth, NH: Heinemann.

Revising Teaching: Drawing, Writing, and Learning with My Students

Elizabeth Olbrych

The author describes her use of a writers'/artists' workshop with her fourth-grade students. The workshop structure provided opportunities to share writing and artwork, participate in read-aloud discussions, and engage in personal responses to books read and student writing. Elizabeth is challenged, both as a teacher: (Why is the quality of the kids' work appearing to nose-dive? How much direction should I provide? How can I best facilitate the revision of their pieces?) and as a participant in the workshop activities (How can my own writing and sketching truly capture a sense of place? What strategies can help me achieve my intentions? How can sharing my own struggle and strategies help the students with their work?). The article shares a number of invitations and strategies that can be incorporated into any workshop-focused curriculum.

Portugal

Bom dia
Eating sugary fruit pastries
Under a tilted umbrella
Drinking creamy, sweet galao
At an outdoor café
Seeing a cloud curtain dangle
Over the castelo dos mouros

Boa tarde
Smelling the stale, eerie air
In Evora's Chapel of Bones
Hearing languages mingle
In the cobblestone hills of Sintra
Seeing fishermen mend nets
In the shade of beached boats

From *Primary Voices K–6, 10*(2), Oct. 2001, 10–17.

Boa noite
Eating pork with salty potatoes
By trees dorned with white lights
Smelling grilled sardines
On the docks in Cascais
Seeing fishing boat lights
String the horizon like a city.
Obrigada

This poem evolved as I was setting up an artists'/writers' workshop for my fourth-grade class at the beginning of the year. It started as a series of descriptions and sketches that I kept in my sketch journal as I traveled through Portugal. Over the course of the fall, I experimented with genre, structure, and wording. I used the supports I needed as a writer both to inform my teaching and to set up structures that would help my students grow as writers.

Getting Started

I began our first workshop by reading *All the Places to Love,* by Patricia MacLachlan. It's a picture book with stunning illustrations and detailed descriptions of places. I chose this book to inspire my own art and writing about Portugal, which at this point consisted of quick sketches and lists. After reading, the class and I discussed how the author created a sense of place with her words, and how the illustrator portrayed those images in pictures. I showed them the sketch journal that I kept on my trip and shared my intentions of turning these drafts into a more polished piece of writing and art.

My fourth graders told stories of vacation memories and special places that were significant to them. We started to learn about each other through sharing these stories, and these ideas propelled our work. I invited them to start thinking about their ideas by creating pictures. The act of drawing or painting an image helped students remember details, which put them deeper in touch with the ideas they were exploring. I told them where to find the picture books, art cards, crayons, markers, and colored pencils, and I limited them to these materials at first. It's important to start slowly when introducing new routines and materials so that they are used purposefully.

I gave the class invitations for their work that day. They could draw and write about a vacation memory, a special place, or they could browse the collection of picture books and art cards in the class library for inspiration. (For additional "invitations," see Figure 5.1.) Having a visual to study often helps children who need a concrete model of the image they have in mind. Students could also create their own invitations from their imaginations as long as they led to thoughtful kinds of work. I recorded their plans for the workshop that day on a class list, and they headed off to work.

Figure 5.1.
Invitations to Write:
A Starting List

- Paint your picture with words.
- Where did your imagination/mind go as you made your picture?
- Describe your process in making this picture.
- What did you learn about yourself today as a writer and artist?
- Describe the action in your picture.
- Capture a moment in your picture.
- If you made your picture again, what changes would you make?
- Why did you choose the material that you did for your picture? How would your picture change if you changed the material?
- What's the mood in your picture?
- Tell the story that goes with this picture.

Everyone found inspiration rather quickly. Craig worked on a giraffe from an art card in bright, bold-colored markers. Julia drew a horse from her perspective while riding him. Remy and Adam started separate rainforest pictures, but decided to cut Adam's frog out and glue it into Remy's leafy background. There was a hum of chatter while they drew their stories.

I often sit down next to various groups of students for a short period to work on my own art and writing. This tells them that I am also a writer, artist, and learner. Knowing that these are skills that I use gives children an image of an adult engaged in purposeful work. They can also trust me as a reliable resource for their learning. During this first workshop, I was having a hard time getting started. I wanted to copy a picture of an ancient stone castle in Portugal, and write about how interwoven history and the present day were in the country's landscape. Even though I knew what I wanted to make, the image on the page wasn't matching the image in my mind. I knew this could develop into an important lesson to share with the children. It happens to all artists and writers, and students need to develop strategies for overcoming difficulties in the writing process. I solved my problem by temporarily changing my focus to teacher-researcher, and using the time to learn from the other writers in the room. (Although I always try to work on my own art and writing for a short period, I do spend most of my time during the workshop interacting with children and using my sketch journal as a resource tool.)

I walked around the room with sketch journal in hand to observe my students. I recorded snippets of conversations and descriptions of their work, along with quick sketches of them. This helped me learn about their personal interests and working styles, areas of strength, and areas for instruction. After a 30-minute drawing or writing period, we stopped to write together silently. Taking the time to write silently provides a quiet environment for students who prefer to write without distractions, and also sets the standard that writing is an expectation and a priority. Children learn from the beginning that all artwork must be accompanied by thoughtful writing, and they must choose ideas for picture making with this criterion in mind. We wrote silently for 20 minutes in response to the following invitations I had written on the board:

Describe the place where your picture is set.

Tell how you got your idea for your work today.

Tell the story/memory that goes with your picture.

Other thoughtful choices

At the end of the workshop, we took time to share informally. As they shared, I recorded lines of writing from each piece in my sketch journal. This helped me recall the pieces of writing, and become familiar with the children's styles. I often reread these lines, as well as entire pieces, to plan minilessons for subsequent workshops. During this workshop, I recorded the following excerpts in my journal:

Julie—"The Bird"—As I hide my beak under my blue, green, and yellow feathers, I feel the wind pounding against my face. It's so strong, it could knock me over in one caw. . . .

Willy—"Surfer Castle"—I got my idea of making my sand castle after I almost broke my back. I almost broke it when I rode up a massive 25-foot wave, and it crashed down on me, and my boogie board slammed my upper body. I got the wind knocked out of me and staggered up the beach. I sat out for a while and got the idea of a surfer castle when I saw a great surfer. . . .

Amelie—"Almost Night"—The water shoves the sailboats along. As the water splashes against the shore of the little island, the boats are rising, and it looks like the orange one is in the lead. Colors fill the sky and the sun goes down over the water. I bet the moon is getting ready to come out soon. . . . It's almost time to go inside, but I bet anyone would want to be out here.

Hearing the power of their voices sharing lines reminded me of the importance of children using a physical image to help propel writing. As you can see from their writing, having the opportunity to create artwork before writing helped these children develop the skills of description, reflection, attention to sound and rhythm, and word choice.

There were children who did not share their writing, as I did not, that day. I did tell them about my struggles, how I had realized my piece might need a different focus, and that I had to be brave in taking a risk and trying something new. I wanted the children to see me as a model of a proficient writer, and to learn strategies for drafting and revising writing from observing my process, including challenges and successes.

I wrote these observations and reflections down in my sketch journal while I wrote with the class and after school. I also jotted down the questions that our first writers'/artists' workshop had generated for me as a teacher-researcher:

> I'm wondering where to go with our next workshop. . . . How is the culture of writers'/artists' workshop influencing student writing by the time children reach fourth grade? How important are my personal needs as a writer in designing workshops? Many students in this class seem quite skilled in creating rich images with their words. What I notice is that they need help now structuring these lines into an organized piece of writing. They need to learn to identify the purpose and genre of their work.

Collecting Drafts

Over the next few weeks, we continued to gather drawings and pieces of writing on various topics. Each day, I would share with my class where I was in the process of creating my work on Portugal, how I dealt with challenges, my personal interests, and how I crafted a piece through revision. We shared often and learned about each other as people and writers.

I took notes as I talked with students individually and as a class, and as I studied their collections of art and writing. Then, as I reread the observations that I had recorded in my sketch journal, certain patterns emerged that highlighted places where my students needed help. I based my minilessons on those needs as well as on my needs as a co-writer in the classroom. Through this process, I became increasingly aware of the significance of direct instruction and modeling in a most obvious way.

During the first workshop, Julie had drawn a parrot, and written a story from its point of view. It was a good piece of writing, but she wasn't satisfied. She wasn't sure how to organize her piece or what her point was. These were issues I was dealing with in writing my own piece about Portugal, and I realized that I needed to teach my class how to revise.

At the time, I was reading *Lifetime Guarantees* (Harwayne, 2000) and came across a poem called "Childhood Tracks," by James Berry. I thought the focus on sounds and smells would help me in my work, so I started to brainstorm lists of what I ate, drank, smelled, and heard in Portugal. During drawing time, I worked on copying photographs that captured these moments for me in a concrete way. This helped me remember the little details I had forgotten. I used a structure I learned from Georgia Heard (1998) about creating "rooms for poetry." I made four boxes on a sketch journal page and wrote as specifically as possible what I experienced in Portugal with my senses, one sense per box. I started to draft lines of a poem grouped by sensory experience, choosing lines that recreated Portugal for me:

> Eating succulent porco at Porca
> Eating sweet pastries stuffed with cheese,
> and drizzled with sauce
> Eating sizzling garlic shrimp
> Eating fried bananas with a golden, crispy
> crust and creamy center
> Drinking creamy, sweet galao in the late
> morning under an umbrella
> Smelling the grilled sardines down by the
> docks
> Smelling the hot, salty sea air

I knew I was far from finished, but I also knew I had found the genre and focus for my writing.

To begin the next workshop, I shared how the structure of that poem helped guide my writing about Portugal. I read "Childhood Tracks" to the class, shared the four-room list I had started and the pictures I had been working on, and read the most recent lines of my poem. The children were quick to provide positive feedback, but also suggestions for improving my draft. Children told me which lines created the most complete images for them. They honestly told me that my poem didn't sound like a poem yet. They wondered if I could include any words in Portuguese.

I took their suggestions seriously as co-writers, and reworked my poem during the work period that followed. At the same time, Julie wrote another parrot piece emulating that style. She was much more satisfied with her revised version. I realized that I needed to create more opportunities for students to revisit pieces through explicit teaching and modeling.

Rethinking Structures

By October, I realized that our workshop was not going to run smoothly forever with the same structures and routines. I looked around the workshop one day and saw things that I hadn't noticed. Artwork and writing had taken a nosedive in quality. Students were making quick pictures with little thought or effort, and this directly impacted the quality of their writing. If their drawings reflected little thought or meaning in the act of making them, they could not use pictures to inspire well-crafted pieces of writing. During this time, management was taking up most of my time and energy. I continued to write in my sketch journal to help me think through the problem and work on a solution.

After reflecting, I realized that I had *let* them slip into trite, superficial artwork, which led to lower-quality writing. I had been too hands-off in their choice of topics, not focusing enough on how to work through ideas that are worth the effort. I realize that not every piece of writing that the students or I do is final-draft quality, but it's important that whatever we write is important to us and could potentially lead to something bigger. We had hit a plateau, and the students needed me to step in and redirect them, but I also wanted them to acknowledge the problem themselves.

We devoted some time to examining this issue. I told the class what I had been noticing about the quality of writing and that I thought it directly related to their choices during drawing time. Then I asked the students to tell me where they got the ideas for their best, high-quality writing as I recorded their responses in my sketch journal. Two themes emerged that the class noticed: (1) they had to have a genuine interest in the topic in order for it to lead to thoughtful writing; (2) it helped to have some knowledge of the topic. With these thoughts in mind, we headed into our workshop that day.

I asked students to spend the first 15–20 minutes reviewing pieces already in their portfolios. They needed to write in response to the following questions to evaluate their work at this point in the year:

> What stands out as your best work? What makes this work stand out? Where did these initial ideas come from?
>
> What pieces don't meet your expectations for yourself? Why not?
>
> What can you do about it?
>
> What do you notice about yourself as an artist-writer at this point in fourth grade?

Many students discovered strong qualities in their writing that they wanted to expand upon. Samantha wrote, "I notice that it is easy to write about nature. When I write about nature, it comes out descriptive because you can write about the environment and what sounds you hear, like 'The wind howls or the waves thrash.'" Remy observed, "I usually draw artwork that has action in it, or nonfiction facts to help." Danielle wrote, "A horse in a stall and the river pieces are my best because they are very descriptive, and they help me connect with the outside world." By identifying their strengths, these students were able to expand upon them in future workshops.

Students also noted what the obstacles were for them in the art and writing process. Chelsea wrote, "My Glamour Girls piece didn't meet my expectations because I rushed and didn't work hard on it."

Julia wrote, "I notice that if I'm not writing or drawing about something that I like, or that interests me, that nothing turns out good." Sam problem-solved, "I think I should write more poems because the description comes much easier." Julie reflected, "There's one piece of writing that doesn't meet my expectations because it's a poem, and I was just looking at the picture for things that I could put down, and rhyming words." These written reflections led to helpful class discussions about how to handle unavoidable challenges in writing. Lizzie summed up the experience of many writers facing a block, "It might have just been one of those days where I don't have any good ideas to write about . . . one of those days where I just do the writing to get it over with." This information was crucial for me as a teacher in providing support for students as they grappled with very real, very difficult situations.

After students wrote, they needed to tell me their plans for the rest of the workshop period based on what they had learned during their portfolio review. They made much more thoughtful choices, and their artwork and writing became more detailed, descriptive, and interesting. I learned that I needed to be honest with them, jump in to help solve the issues, and put the responsibility on them to make changes.

I also realized that I needed to require students to produce a final draft piece of writing by a given deadline. I began the process with a discussion of what the word *revision* meant and asked the students to share with me what past experiences they had in revising a picture and piece of writing. We talked about how to choose a piece to revise—that it had to be a piece that needed improvement, but one that you cared enough about to work on for a long time. Students selected pieces to revise and shared their intentions with me through a written reflection. Vivianna wrote, "In the mud piece, I didn't exactly put it the way I wanted. I wanted a memory, but it came out too much like a description." Devin chose to revise one of his favorite pieces and fill in more details to make it a descriptive story. Zach chose to work his own description into the form of a poem.

Lizzie chose her lobster piece because "I just didn't know what else to choose." We looked at her work and realized that she had a series of lobster pictures. Each picture brought back a memory of a different age in her life. She decided to rewrite her lobster piece into a poem for two voices. One voice was Lizzie at age three, and the other was the older Lizzie at age five. Drawing the pictures helped her discover stories to write.

I also worked to meet the writing deadline and conferred with students to advise them on their pieces. During minilessons, I modeled strategies such as highlighting lines that created the strongest images, drawing a subject from different perspectives or in different materials, and choosing a genre. I asked them to rely on the expertise of their peers while I was busy with a student. They learned how to ask questions that help writers clarify a point, and to give a suggestion in a supportive tone.

Two weeks after they had chosen their revision pieces, students were ready with edited pieces of writing and artwork that supported their pieces, and we celebrated with a class share. My writing and art had become my vehicle for teaching in that they provided a model for students as they learned about the process of revision. Our conversations—writer-to-writer, artist-to-artist—led students to take themselves and their work seriously.

References   Harwayne, S. (2000). *Lifetime guarantees: Toward ambitious literacy teaching.* Portsmouth, NH: Heinemann.

Heard, G. (1998). *Awakening the heart: Exploring poetry in elementary and middle school.* Portsmouth, NH: Heinemann.

MacLachlan, P. (1994). *All the places to love.* New York: Scholastic.

Resource Box 5

Flexible Structures in a Writers/Artists Workshop Minilesson

At the beginning of each workshop, spend time with the whole class to give explicit instruction in a writing skill or strategy, or in developing classroom expectations and routines. Components of this time may include:
- Sharing writing and artwork from children's literature, student and teacher work, and the work of professional authors and artists
- Read-aloud and discussion of a picture book or poem. Examine elements of style and craft in writing and illustrating
- Personal responses, reflections on literature, and student sharing
- Explicit instruction in skills, techniques, literary elements, and conventions
- Directions in use of materials, reviewing routines and expectations
- Quick-writes to inspire thinking and promote experimentation with new conventions or ideas
- List of choices of topics and materials
- Status of the class—recording student plans for work

Workshop Time (independent or collaborative work)
- Students and teacher draw and write. They work in their sketch journals or collections of loose work held in portfolios. The teacher works alongside the students on his or her own work, has conversations with students about their ideas, provides instruction to individuals and small groups, observes and records notes on student work and conversations.
- Response groups meet to give one another updates on their writing progress, positive feedback, and constructive criticism.

Quiet Writing-Only Period (used as necessary with individual classes)
- Independent writing period provides some students with an environment that helps them focus and craft their pieces.
- Invitations to write are listed on the board. Students may choose from the leads or follow an idea of their own.

Sharing
To help build and sustain a writing community, have students share in a variety of ways. Response groups meet on a regular basis to share recent work. Sharing at the end of our workshop takes on a form of its own.
- Students share a line or excerpt from their work that day to build writing community and to see one another as resources. This should be kept brief. Longer sharing should be saved for minilessons, response group meetings, and final draft celebrations.

6 Units of Study in the Writing Workshop

Isoke Titilayo Nia

The author explores the use of units of study—fiction, memoir, and essay—in the writing workshop. Organizing study in this way helped her students pay close attention to particular genres and to discover their capacities as writers. This structure also helped make clear the necessity of collecting, and immersing learners in, best examples of a particular genre as they are asked to create instances of that genre themselves. Isoke and her colleagues learned that organizing this kind of study across the school year was a clear benefit to this community of writers, resulting in more and better writing.

In writing workshops across the world, teachers are struggling with the repetitiveness of teaching the writing process. On their walls, they have charts that show the steps of the process in linear or circular shapes. They march their students progressively through these steps, time and time again, like a machine. Faced with the quandary, "What am I to teach?" in the seemingly endless cycle, they reluctantly answer, "I guess I teach how to do each of these steps better one more time or teach random minilessons on whatever comes up on a given day." As a study group, we wanted a better answer than that to this curriculum question, and so we searched together for an organizing structure for our writing workshops. We wanted to plan units of study that would carry us across the year with our students.

A unit of study in writing is not unlike a unit of study in science or social studies. It is a line of inquiry—a road of curriculum, a trail of teaching, an excursion of knowing something about writing. It is some big thing that you and your class are digging into over time. For several weeks you plan minilessons and lines of inquiry that allow your students to become actively involved in creating the curriculum around the unit of study. If some outside force is requiring you to study something—say, "personal narrative" for the fourth-grade writing test—you turn that requirement into a unit of study on memoir that actively involves students as real writers engaged in inquiry.

From *Primary Voices K–6, 8*(1), Aug. 1999, 3–9.

Planning the Year

School years are made of time, and so when we started we looked for ways we might wrap these inquiries around the approximately 180 days of our school year. We imagined the school calendar in increments of time, each lasting approximately three to eight weeks. Next, we had to think about what we might study. As we thought about our teaching and our experiences in writing workshop, we decided there were many possibilities for studies that might help our students grow as writers. We generated the following list of possibilities for units of study:

> genre studies: fiction, memoir, poetry, essay, etc.
>
> the writing process itself, from idea to publication
>
> individual parts of the process, such as revision, editing, or gathering in the writing notebook
>
> living the writerly life
>
> collaboration (writing in partnerships and other groupings)
>
> a particular author
>
> the craft of writing: genre, structure, sound, language system
>
> difficulty—what are students struggling with?
>
> using a writer's notebook throughout the process
>
> stamina in the writing workshop (helping students develop muscles to make writing better)

This list helped us envision what a whole year's worth of study might include. Each of us began the process of making important curricular decisions about what units we would include in our planning for the year and where we would place these units on the timeline of our study.

We first considered units of genre studies. The focus of a genre study is on a particular type of writing and its attributes. We began with genre study because it was what we thought we knew (though we would find out we had a lot to learn as we went along). Genre studies seemed available. We had read about them in our mentor books on the teaching of writing by Randy Bomer (1995), Jo Ann Hindley (1996), and Lucy Calkins (1994), who wrote, "We regard genre studies as fundamental enough to shape our curriculum around them. We find that when an entire class inquires into a genre, it is life-giving" (p. 363). We remembered writing poems and stories as children, and, as avid readers, we knew lots of texts in different genres. So genre studies seemed a logical place to start and they seemed like units of study that could sustain us for much of the year.

Organizing for Genre Study

We learned through experience that regardless of the type of genre study we were having, the organization of the study was very similar. We organized a study of poetry in much the same way as we organized a study of fiction. The content was different, but the structure of the study was basically the same, as shown in the following structural frame for a genre study.

Genre Study Steps

Best-Guess Gathering

Immersion

Sifting

Second Immersion

Selecting Touchstone Texts

Touchstone Try-Its

Writing

Reflecting/Assessing

Best-Guess Gathering

When I get an image of what best-guess gathering looks like in a classroom, I am reminded of the treasure hunts that I participated in at the Brooklyn Museum as a child. I remember getting a clipboard and a short yellow pencil and then being let loose to find a list of treasures. I remember some children lagging behind because the clues on the clipboard didn't seem to be enough, and sometimes the instructors would say more about each clue before they sent us off. But most times it was just the clues and us. It wasn't as if the instructors thought the clues were really all we had to go on. They knew we knew more. We were museum students. We were junior members of the museum and were expected to know something about it. Our monthly treasure hunts gave us a sense of ownership, a sense of "this is our museum." When I found the treasure—the museum was mine.

In best-guess gathering, the teacher and the students go into their world on a treasure hunt and bring to the classroom what they think are examples of the genre. Teachers must decide how much they want to say to prepare their students for the hunt. Many teachers do not define the genre at all, choosing instead to allow the definition of the genre to emerge from the gathered texts. They trust that students have in their minds an image of the genre and they want them to use this image to truly make a best guess. Other teachers might choose to say more—to give their students an image of the genre before they go out to gather. In the genre studies offered in *Primary Voices K–6*, you will notice how each teacher makes this decision in his or her own way.

While most teachers invite their students in on the gathering, this part of the study can be as individual as a single teacher and an evening in the library. It can also be as large as announcements over the loudspeaker to an entire school population: "Class 2-499 is studying poetry. Please help them with their study by placing your favorite poem in the envelope outside their classroom door!" No matter how teachers choose to approach this step, they should wind up with a huge pile of "stuff"—of best-guess genre examples—that have been gathered.

Immersion   As the material comes into the room, the teacher and students are reading it together, immersing themselves in all their best-guess "stuff." As they choose interesting examples to read, they are beginning to pay attention to the sound and look of the genre and noticing the writing they admire. They are sorting the stuff into piles— categorizing in ways that help them define the genre. I have often asked students at this stage of a genre study to put things in piles that help them say smart things about the genre. I have to trust them to do this. I have to trust that everything they say is important and will somehow push the learning forward.

Around all the sorting and reading there must be a lot of talking. The students will use their talk to create a working definition of the genre as they notice generalities across examples. They will also notice so much more than they would if the definition of the genre had been handed to them in the beginning.

Sifting   After students have had time (three to four days) to look closely at the pieces of writing, they are ready to begin sifting. This is a process of selecting specific texts that will carry the genre study forward. We usually sift texts out for three reasons:

The text is not an example of the genre.

The text is an example of the genre, but it is not like what we will write. Because of such variety within genres, we must make a decision about what kinds of texts we will write. We keep only these kinds in our sifting.

The text belongs to the genre, and it is like what we will write, but it just isn't good writing. We just don't like it so we take it out. This is also when I'd remove anything that might not be appropriate content for the class to use as a model.

As you are sifting, remember that the world of literature is large. There is no reason for a single piece of literature that is not the best to be included in the study.

Second Immersion/ Selecting Touchstone Texts

Again the students need to immerse themselves in the genre, but this time they are looking at pieces that are exactly like the kind of writing they will be doing. This immersion has so much to do with the ears, with getting the sound of the genre inside the students. It is when students begin to look at the details of the pieces of writing. The beautiful beginnings and endings. The pictures that make you want to cry. During this immersion the teacher is looking for a touchstone text for the class, and the students are looking for mentor pieces for themselves. How do they know when they find them? When a piece seems to jump out of someone's small pile and literally scream his or her name followed by the names of all the students in the class, then that student or teacher has selected a touchstone text (see Figure 6.1).

Touchstone Try-Its

The touchstone text for the class is made available for every student. For several days students will read and talk about the text, discussing anything they notice about the writing. The focus of the inquiry at this point is to try to figure out how the writer went about the writing. Students discuss decisions they think the writers of touchstone texts have made about such things as what to include in plot, or whether to repeat a word for effect, or which punctuation to use. The purpose of this close study and the conversations around it is to help students envision new possibilities for their own writing.

In minilessons and conferences, the teacher is asking students to "try it," try out the different writing moves they have noticed professional authors using. The touchstone try-it is safe, even playful. Students try things in notebooks and drafts just to see how they sound. If they like some writing a touchstone author has helped them to do, they may include what they have tried in their actual publications. The try-its especially help students who are reluctant to revise, giving them a range of options to explore during revision. During a conference, a teacher might help a student try a writing move out loud so the student can hear how the writing would sound. The teacher is alert for places in notebooks and drafts where it might make sense to suggest try-its to students.

Writing

Students *write* throughout the genre study. They are collecting entries in their notebooks, nurturing seed ideas for projects, playing with touchstone try-its, publishing pieces for their own reasons, and so on. In the step-by-step structural frame for genre study that I outlined above, the writing step refers to the drafting, revising, and editing of a published piece in the genre under study. The writing time for this is fairly short (usually about six days) because of all the genre study work that has come before it. There is an additional time period for the actual publishing of this piece of work if it is to be

Figure 6.1.
Characteristics of
Touchstone Texts

Selecting Touchstone Texts

You have read the text and you love it.
"You" means the teacher! You love this text so much that you think just by reading it your students will fall instantly in love with it. Your love will be contagious.

You and your students have talked about the text a lot as readers first.
No piece of literature was written to be taken apart or dissected. It was written to speak to us and to help us change the lives we lead. Our first response to a piece of literature should be as readers. Talk first and talk well before you begin to dissect any piece of writing for your study.

You find many things to teach in the text.
The text feels full—teaching full. You see so much that you can teach using just this one piece of literature.

You can imagine talking about the text for a very long time.
Make sure that the text you choose can carry the weight of constant talk and examination.

Your entire class can have access to the text.
A touchstone no one can touch won't work. The piece you choose must be short enough to be put on an overhead, make photocopies from, or have multiple copies of the book for no more than five or six students to share at a time.

Your students can read the text independently or with some support.
Because you are going to invest so much time and talk in this one piece of literature, you don't really need to worry about whether every child can read the text independently. This text is going to come with lots of support.

The text is a little more sophisticated than the writing of your best students.
You want every child to have to work to write like this author. Make sure you choose something that will be challenging. Trust the literature and study time to help students meet this challenge.

The text is written by a writer you trust.
When your back is up against a wall, have some old standbys to reach for. Have a few authors you know "by heart" and whose work you really trust.

The text is a good example of writing of a particular kind (genre).
There are some pieces of writing that are almost textbook examples of a genre. Look for these and save them *forever* because they so well represent what the genre is all about.

The text is of the genre that we are studying.
For first-time genre studies, try to keep the genre "pure"—meaning if you are studying memoir for the first time, you might not include memoir in the form of poetry or song. You might look only at narrative memoir that first time.

You have read the text and loved it.
And just in case you forgot, you have read it and fallen so deeply in love with this piece of writing that you feel privileged to use it in teaching. You run into your minilessons with joy because you have under your arm one of your favorites. Your love of the text is fuel for your study.

presented in a particular way, such as in a class magazine or in an anthology of poetry.

Reflecting/ Assessing

After any study (genre or otherwise) the teacher and students should spend some time reflecting on and assessing their work. They should look at both their processes and their products. This assessment can be as simple as a narrative—having students answer a question, or several questions, about their work:

How did going through this study feel?

What was hard for you?

What do you think about your finished piece?

Assessment may also be as demanding as a rubric created jointly by teacher and students. The assessment tool that you choose should reflect the sophistication of your students. I try to begin the year with the narrative question assessment, then move to checklists and rubrics, and end my year with a combination of both. Whichever tool you use should always lead to more talk among you and your students. Your goal is not just to have students complete writing projects. You want them to really understand these projects, and you want to use their understandings to revise your teaching.

The beauty of this frame for a genre study is that it can be used to organize so much good teaching in the writing workshop. The driving force behind this kind of study is the principle of immersion, the idea that students and teachers need to be deep readers of whatever kind of writing they are learning to do. And equally beautiful is the fact that you can be a learner alongside your students. Beginning a study means trusting the learner part of you. You don't need to know everything there is to know about a genre to do a genre study with your students. It is good to have some background knowledge—which you can acquire by reading examples of the genre, books by writers about writing, and books on the teaching of writing—but the best knowledge comes from active involvement in the study with your class.

Benefits of Study in the Classroom

Units of study are essential to the writing workshop because without them, what is the work of the workshop on a day-to-day basis? Like a learning map you and your students chart together, your studies create a year's worth of curriculum for the workshop that exposes students to new possibilities as writers.

Units of study help to set the pace for your workshop. They add quality and consistency that both students and teachers need in a workshop setting. When study is valued and arranged with skill and care in a school year, a teacher can both expose her students to many genres and have them become experts in a few. When units of study are planned around writing issues other than genre, students are exposed to a wide range of helpful curriculum for their writing lives. Smaller studies (mini-inquiries) of one week or so can be carefully placed between longer studies when they are necessary to meet student needs. These small studies create a sense of continuity in the work.

Many teachers have found it useful to develop a calendar for units of study during the year. One example is presented in Resource Box 6 at the end of this essay. Notice the units selected and the length of time allotted for each.

This calendar becomes public knowledge. It is the learning map that our students and we will use. Publication dates are spread out liberally across the calendar to ensure that we will publish often and to give us something to live toward in our studies. This is the quality that we strive for in our work together: planfulness. It is something like how we live our social lives. We plan a social calendar with specific dates and occasions, but we always make sure we leave room for the unexpected—the last-minute tickets to a great play or the dinner invitation to the new restaurant in town.

Teachers have to think of curriculum calendars in much the same way: We learned that we couldn't map out the whole year in August. We learned that to live toward study meant we had to plan several times a year. We had to look at our calendars and our students often and reshape our plans. We learned to trust our August thinking and our November thinking and to let one nourish the other. A part of that learning was to accept that we couldn't really know what our whole calendar would look like until we got to June. It wasn't that we weren't thinking about June much earlier in the year. We just realized that we had to remain open to the possibilities that June might bring.

We also learned to take time (in August and at several points during the school year) to follow these lines of thinking:

Can I imagine how I'd like the work to go?

What would I like my students to get from a study?

Why am I tackling this hard work?

Can I imagine a time span?

What are the structures I need to exist in my classroom to make this type of learning possible? How can we get them in?

How important are the writing notebooks going to be?

What supplies and literature need to exist in this classroom to make our work possible, and where or how are we going to acquire them?

What lessons will I need to teach? (Leave room for some you can't imagine yet. Pay close attention to what is happening in your class. Take good notes. Study your conferences. *Then,* ask yourself again, "What lessons will I need to teach?")

With whom will I share this learning journey? (Don't travel alone. It's easier with a friend by your side.)

We reflected on these questions periodically as a group and as individuals. They helped us know what needed to come next on our planful journey through the curriculum year.

Raising the Level of Work

We have found that sharing with our students this sort of "calendar approach" to planning for the writing workshop—setting publication dates and making clear what will be studied—has raised both the production level and the quality of writing our students produce. The predictable immersion part of any study of writing helps students learn to read like writers. Over time, reading like writers through thoughtful, well-planned units of study helps students develop an excellent sense of what good writing is so that they can identify and emulate it wherever they find it in the world.

Units of study in the writing workshop also allow students to discover the kinds of writers they are. The child who loves poetry will shine during the poetry study and cringe (perhaps) during the nonfiction genre study but will have many spaces in between to write in the genre that she or he wishes. The beauty of genre study is that it never removes a child's right to choose a topic. Though students may gather to study a very particular kind of writing, they are always writing about topics they have chosen themselves. The studies strengthen their sense of craft and help them envision all the possibilities that exist for their ideas.

Note

All of the writers included in this issue are members of a Writing Leadership Group within the Teachers College Reading and Writing Project, Columbia University, Leadership Project. This group is led by Isoke Titilayo Nia and funded by a grant written by the projects director, Lucy Calkins, from Morgan Guaranty Trust Company of New York.

References

Bomer, R. (1995). *Time for meaning: Crafting literate lives in middle and high school.* Portsmouth, NH: Heinemann.

Calkins, L. (1994). *The art of teaching writing.* Portsmouth, NH: Heinemann.

Hindley, J. (1996). *In the company of children.* York, ME: Stenhouse.

Resource Box 6

Sample Yearlong Curriculum Chart		
Dates of Publication/ Celebration	Units of Study	Types of Publication
1. September 25	Living the Writerly Life	varied genres
2. October 23	Memoir	memoir in prose form
3. November 30	Short Story (Fiction)	short story
4. December 23	Craft Study	varied genres
5. January 10	Revision	turning over a piece previously published
6. February 25	Nonfiction	feature article, essay, or editorial
7. March 15	Using Notebooks to Make Our Writing Better	varied genres
8. March 31	Structure	varied genres
9. April 30	Memoir	memoir as poetry or vignette
10. May 20	Literary Response (Writing in Response to Reading)	book review and literary criticism (two pieces)
11. June 20	Revision	turning over a piece previously published

Resource Box 7

Blank Chart to Use for Planning		
Dates of Publication/ Celebration	Units of Study	Types of Publication
1.		
2.		
3.		
4.		
5.		
6.		
7.		
8.		
9.		
10.		
11.		

Reflection Point

> Reflect on the following questions with regards to your own classroom.
>
> What ways have you found to make curriculum relevant and also attend to curricular mandates?
>
> In what ways do you access the repertoire of experiences that your students bring to the classroom from their home communities?
>
> What meaning-making systems do you include as regular features of your curriculum? Which of these come from your students' communities, families, or cultures?
>
> What meaning-making systems do you find difficult to include as a regular feature of your curriculum?

III Practices That Support Inquiry

What we study is just as important as how we study it. In the past, the research or inquiry component of a language arts program focused on helping children use reading and writing to investigate, to ask questions, and to study the world around them. An inquiry-based curriculum focuses on developing children as inquirers by teaching them to observe things closely, to ask questions, to engage in conversation, and to reflect on their learning.

Over the years, however, primarily through research conducted by teachers in their classrooms, we have learned that to be relevant, inquiry has to be rooted in the lives of learners and the communities in which they live, and based on topics about which they are passionate. (See, for example, B. Comber, "Classroom Explorations in Critical Literacy," *Australian Journal of Language and Literacy, 16*(1), 1993, pp. 73–83; J. O'Brien, "Experts in Smurfland," in M. Knobel and A. Healy [Eds.], *Critical Literacy in the Primary Classroom*, Newton, NSW: Primary English Teaching Association, 1998, pp. 47–68; and V. Vasquez, *Negotiating Critical Literacies with Young Children*, Mahwah, NJ: Erlbaum, 2004; "Classroom Inquiry into the Incidental Unfolding of Social Justice Issues: Seeking Out Possibilities in the Lives of Learners," in S. Boran and B. Comber [Eds.], *Critiquing Whole Language and Classroom Inquiry*, Urbana, IL: NCTE, 2001, pp. 200–215; and "Constructing a Critical Curriculum with Young Children," in B. Comber and A. Simpson [Eds.], *Negotiating Critical Literacies in Classrooms*, Mahwah, NJ: Erlbaum, 2001, pp. 55–66.) How such inquiry connects to defined curriculum may present a challenge, but it is one we are willing to engage because of the understanding that relevant learning begins here. Most of all, we are interested in the action that results when inquirers position themselves with new knowledge, experience, and commitment.

What this means is that we need to create spaces in our classrooms for learners to explore everyday issues of personal relevance to them, whether they be relationships with family and friends, a love of nature, softball, music, or math, the fun of exploring old city neighborhoods and new technologies, or realities such as bullying, sexual identity, AIDS, drug use, and racism. At the Center for Inquiry in Indianapolis, for example, students have inquired into what Indianapolis looks like through the lenses of art, music, and dance. Others have explored discrimination through collecting data on how long it takes African Americans to get waited on in contrast to European American customers at a local fashion mall. These topics were all generated during class conversations. Students' inquiries into these topics as well as their culminating projects represent a new set of social practices for language arts teachers: using reading and writing as tools for making a difference in our world. In this section you will read about three such communities of inquirers. (For further examples of children taking social action, see C. Paul, "Using Technology to Research Issues of Gender in the Language Arts Classroom, *School Talk, 8*[3], 2003, p. 2–4; V. Vasquez, "Building Equitable Communities: Taking Social Action in a Kindergarten Classroom," *Talking Points, 9*[2], 1998, pp. 3–6; and V. Vasquez and K. Egawa, eds., "Everyday Texts/Everyday Literacies," *School Talk, 8*[1], 2002, pp.1–8.)

More than ever, the future is about building curriculum from students' own issues and ideas, as well as supporting them in the pursuit of their questions, and to that end the articles chosen for this section focus on practices that support inquiry. Learners often learn the most about inquiry by observing their teachers as inquirers, constantly engaged in research, deconstructing and decoding the world around them, and using this information to challenge and address inequities. For instance, in the Craviotto, Heras, and Espíndola article, the fourth graders and the university students engage in similar processes as they explore the challenges faced by immigrants and how those new to a community gain a solid footing. The demonstrations teachers provide are invaluable.

We have also chosen these articles because we think their work has made a difference, both in the lives of these learners and in their communities. The details for accomplishing this multifaceted task are uncovered through articles in which we see students and teachers become what Karen Smith describes as "co-investigators," as topics of inquiry advance through conscious decision making and planning.

The elements of an inquiry process, and more specifically of the instances of inquiry that follow in the articles, are shown in the graphics labeled A–D on pages 71–72.

The articles included in this section are "Bringing Children and Literature Together in the Elementary Classroom," by K. Smith, "Linking Authenticity and Advocacy in Assessment to Inclusion," by T. Enguídanos, and "Cultures of the Fourth-Grade Bilingual Classroom," by E. Craviotto, A. I. Heras, and J. Espíndola.

A

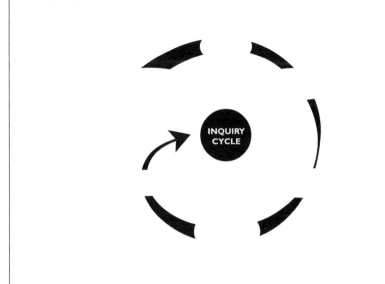

Connection → Invitation → Investigation → Valuation → Action

B

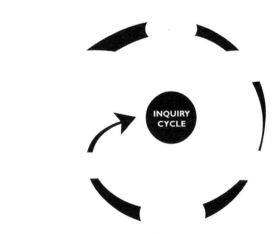

Karen Smith
Literature Study as Inquiry

Read widely and demonstrate response → follow interests → entertain multiple
perspectives → share responses → expand genre experience

C

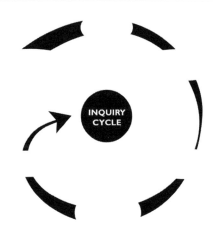

Tomás Enguídanos
Assessment as Inquiry

Immerse in data → identify strengths and celebrate successes → assess
access and equity → establish families as advocates → build collaborative
relationships in schools

D

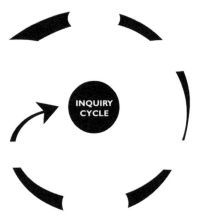

Eileen Craviotto, Ana Inés Heras, and Javier Espíndola
Community Study as Inquiry

Identify questions and collaborators → investigate challenges → immerse in
practice → compare data to key research → reposition for new work

Bringing Children and Literature Together in the Elementary Classroom

Karen Smith

The author describes her former work in a fifth- and sixth-grade classroom using literature as a way of exploring the human condition, to understand that there are many worldviews and that no single one constitutes the standard against which others should be judged. In doing so she taught her students to move beyond their own rendering of a text and consider alternative interpretations.

I t is November 15, and all 32 fifth and sixth graders are busily engaged in meaningful work. Seven students are in the reading corner. This is their day to be "rug readers," a title affectionately bestowed on them by a group of students who developed a plan allowing everyone a weekly time to spread out on the rug and read. Tomás and Martin laugh their way through a beat-up copy of *Mad*. Juan has *Sports Illustrated for Kids* in his lap, apparently planning to turn to it as soon as he finishes reading his superhero comic book. Sabrina and Martha snuggle together in the beanbag chair, reading books by Cynthia Voigt, their favorite author. And Mary, whose head is resting on a pillow in Sabrina's lap, is lost in the world of Terabithia.

In another corner, four pairs of students practice reading aloud to one another from picture books written in Spanish. They're preparing oral readings for their second-grade partners. They know that to read well orally they have to rehearse, so they're both listening to and evaluating one another for fluency, expression, and clarity. Yolanda, Robert, Jorge, Sergio, Marcela, and Danny are creating a mural that will represent their rendering of *Shadow of a Bull* (Wojciechowska, 1964). They discuss the size of the mural and what medium they will use to create it. A fourth group is gathered around

From *Primary Voices K–6, 3*(2), Apr. 1995, 22–32.

a table reading and discussing *Let the Circle Be Unbroken* (Taylor, 1981). The previous week I had been a part of this group and we had read *Roll of Thunder, Hear My Cry* (Taylor, 1975). Now they're reading its sequel, independent of me. The remaining six students make their way to the round table with books and contracts in hand. We are about to meet for a literature study session.

Promoting Independence

These students are confident and serious because they know how to work independently and how to respond appropriately in each situation. I help them learn these things during September and October, when we spend time each day engaging in literary events and then talking about specific behaviors that contributed to the success or failure of each situation. We discuss what went well, and why. We also talk about what didn't go well and come up with ways we can improve next time. I introduce them to a range of response modes (art, music, drama, etc.); usually, I begin with art. Students select a picture book and respond to it using some art form. To give students an idea of the variety of projects possible and the quality of work expected, I share projects completed by former students. The first two days, the students immerse themselves in picture books. The third day, they (alone or in pairs) pick one picture book to respond to. They organize their time on a form that asks them to list whom they will work with, what they plan to create (a diorama, a mural, an abstract rendition of the story, etc.), what materials they will need, where they will get the materials, and where they will work. The form also has a section that asks students to note what worked well and one thing they could have done to make things better. They decide how much time they will need, and spend the next two to five days completing the project. At this point, students turn in their organizational forms, which are evaluated along with the project itself.

We spend about ten minutes at the end of each session discussing what they did and how they proceeded. For example, cleanup is almost always an issue with art projects, so we think through several ways to handle it. If students are working in pairs, they may choose to assign specific tasks for each to do: one student cleans the paint jars and brushes and the other cleans the area. Sharing solutions is important because it presents a range of possibilities for students to consider as they listen to what worked for others. If students have trouble working independently, I meet with them individually, and we talk through why they are having a problem and what goals they will set to take care of it. My objective is not to punish students but to find strategies that will help them be successful. I always follow up the next day to see if their behavior matches their goals. If not, we keep brainstorming and developing new strategies until we find something that works. After everyone has finished an art project, I move to a different form of response, usually drama and music, following basically the same procedures.

Every day after lunch, we have silent reading time that we call "just reading." During this time block, we read and share. Students choose their own books; the only requirement is that it must be a literature book (fiction or nonfiction). There is no quiz over what is read, nor are students required to respond in any way except to talk briefly to a classmate. I encourage them to share with different partners each day. Students spend 35 minutes reading and 10 minutes sharing. This sharing time is important: It makes students think about what they read, it entices other students to read the same book, and it creates a place for us to come together and think and talk as a community of readers.

"Rug reading" begins during this block of time in September and October. Decisions about who gets to read on the rug and when have to be resolved anew each year. Usually a group is assigned to set some guidelines, and then these guidelines are implemented and evaluated for a week or two until the group comes up with a set that works. After several revisions, one group resolved the reading corner problem by creating a chart that listed the students in groups of six next to the day of the week they could read on the rug. Next to the chart was a set of rules: (1) You can read on the rug only on your designated day. If you don't want to read in the reading area, that's okay, but you can't let someone else take your place. (2) You are free to read any text in the classroom library (i.e. magazines, joke books, comic books, etc.) or anything that has been approved by the teacher. [This is unlike the rules for other students, who are required to read books.] (3) You cannot disrupt other students on the rug. [If you do, you must leave and read silently at your desk.] (4) You must straighten up the area before you leave. [Otherwise, you lose your rug privilege the following week.]

I play two important roles during this time block: I read with the students and discuss my reading with a partner, thus establishing myself as a member of this reading community. (I always have at least four novels on my desk and often talk with the students about other books I am reading at home.) I also observe students as they read silently, noting patterns of behavior that seem to keep them from enjoying silent reading.

Dealing with Problems and Distractions

Students who already enjoy reading are left alone. They select a novel from a large array of books; find a comfortable place where they can read without interruption; and at the end of the period they record the title of their book and the pages read on a reading record form and talk to a classmate about what they read. Less interested or less able readers often have trouble seeing themselves as readers. These are the students who distract other students; start a new book every day; read the same pages over and over again; or watch the clock, counting minutes until silent reading time is over. One by one, I meet with them and ask them to talk to me about what they are experiencing during this time. I make inquiries into their history as readers, asking why they think they have trouble reading, why they think it is important to read, if they ever read a book they liked, and so on. They usually tell me their frustration with little probing. Tomás, for example, described how he looked at every word on a page and turned every page in a book, yet he didn't know a thing he'd read. Other students admit they have never read an entire book. Again, I work with these students individually to find strategies that help them overcome these obstacles. We become co-investigators in solving the problem.

If a student is not reading as effectively or efficiently as I think he or she should be, I use the short version of the miscue analysis inventory (Goodman, Watson, and Burke, 1987) to gather information. Together we consider the types and level of miscues being made and what they tell us about the student's reading strategies. If a student is a proficient reader but doesn't like to read, I use other means of support. For example, children who have a hard time keeping their minds on what they read often benefit from sketching interesting or important ideas as they read. I recommend folding a piece of newsprint in quarters for sketch paper. Students then read a short section and sketch a part they find interesting. I do the same and then we compare and talk about why we picked what we did. There are times when we are amazed that one of us has drawn something that the other person didn't remember happening in the story; at other times, we find that both of us picked the same event or character to sketch. Some students need to do this for only a book or two. Others rely on this process for several weeks. They seem to know when they no longer need it and do away with it on their own.

Still other students have problems finding a book they want to read. I encourage these students to read with a classmate. After the two have agreed on a book, they read and share together until they finish it. If possible, I read the same book so I can support them by sharing insights, providing previews of things to come, or helping to sort out parts they find confusing. I talk with students often to see how things are working out and how they are doing. I acknowledge all progress (no matter how small) by calling parents or reporting to former teachers (who always manage to seek out these students and congratulate them on their success).

Figure 7.1.
Susie's Note to the Student
of the Week

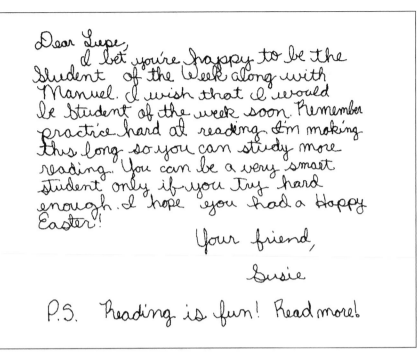

Dear Lupe,
    I bet you're happy to be the Student of the Week along with Manuel. I wish that I would be Student of the week soon. Remember practice hard at reading. I'm making this long so you can study more reading. You can be a very smart student only if you try hard enough. I hope you had a Happy Easter!

Your friend,

Susie

P.S. Reading is fun! Read more!

I want students to understand that being a reader counts. It carries status. Reading three books at once or going to the public library on your own are acts that are important and get noted. Reading three chapters ahead of assigned pages makes you worthy of public acknowledgment by classmates and the teacher alike (Smith, 1993). Because I value reading, students learn to value each other as readers and receive recognition for their reading acts. When other teachers visit our classroom, students often introduce each other by pointing out reading behaviors. Sara is the student who always reads the last chapter first. Efrin is our historical fiction buff. John finally moved away from sports and into fantasy books. Discussing the merits of reading even showed up in a personal note written by a classmate to our Student of the Week (see Figure 7.1).

By the middle of October, students are usually able to act independently: they know how to prepare and participate in buddy reading; they can respond to books using art, music, and drama; and they have settled into silent reading. This independence frees me to work intensively with small groups of students, shifting my focus from creating routines that promote independence to developing students' abilities to respond to literature in deeper and more meaningful ways.

Supporting More Complex Responses

I want students to appreciate literature as aesthetic experience and grow in their ability to respond to it in more sophisticated ways. I also want them to value literature for the roles it can play in their lives. I believe that literature entertains, that it is a wonderful way to spend time; it provides a context for exploring the human condition, helping us to understand who we are and why we exist; and it helps us recognize that there are many worldviews and that no single one constitutes the standard against which others can or should be judged (Smith, 1995). These beliefs have an impact on the response stance I want students to take. I want them to bring to bear on each reading their worldviews, experiences, and concerns. In addition, I want them to learn to move beyond their own rendering of a text and consider alternative and opposing interpretations of the same text.

By mid-October, most of the students value literature as entertainment. They enjoy reading and freely choose to read during and out of class. They have experienced the emotional and imaginative pull of a good story, and recognized the pleasure of being carried to other places and involved in the lives of other people. Also by mid-October, they have been introduced to a particular way of thinking and talking about story. During read-aloud time, when I finish reading a chapter, short story, or picture book, I ask students to sit up straight and get ready to share the thoughts and feelings they experienced while I was reading. Often these responses are about people or events the students either liked or disliked. I accept all responses as important. Some students hesitate to share thoughts and feelings, so when they risk a response, I always acknowledge their contribution. Other students, who are more confident responders, are sometimes asked to substantiate their responses. This often results in personal stories that they call on to make connections to what an author is saying.

I usually make sure some time is spent attending specifically to the story world. Story worlds provide a context for sorting out our thoughts and feelings about a particular aspect of life. I rely on the basic concept and elements of story to help shape our conversation. Leland Jacobs's (1980) notion of story-characters coping in terms of quest sets the stage for this talk. This framework focuses our attention on the characters we meet in stories and on the tensions they are coping with. I ask students to attend to book characters with the same recognition and concern they give (or should give) new acquaintances in their daily lives. Basic story elements—character, place, point of view, time, mood, and extended metaphor (Peterson & Eeds, 1990)—fall into place as students work to make sense of the characters they meet. I never directly teach elements of literature; they emerge naturally as children begin talking about story. What I do, however, is build on students' responses using the elements if I think it will enrich their current understandings. For example, when the class was talking about the tensions that exist between M. C. Higgins and his father in the story *M. C. Higgins, the Great* (Hamilton, 1974), I responded by talking about how much of the tension was related to place. I wanted the students to see that the more insight we gained into Sarah's Mountain (a place named after M. C.'s great-grandmother and deeply cherished by his father), the more we would understand the relationship between M. C. and his dad. Some students saw the connections; others did not. I never worry about whether they "get it." The students who do make the connection often start considering the significance of place in other stories. The students who don't make the connection will have plenty of other opportunities during the year to see the interactions between characters and place.

Besides demonstrating response to literature using a particular literary element, I also name the element or literary device when a student grounds his or her response in it, but doesn't know the word for it. When one of the students voiced amazement that the story of M. C. Higgins took place in a very short time period (two days, to be exact), another student, Alonso, pointed out that we really understood more because the author "told stories about M. C.'s grandmother from 100 years ago." I validated Alonso's insight by noting that what the author had done was use a literary device called flashback and corroborated his response by pointing out specific ways the flashbacks enriched our understanding of the father's tie to the mountain and his deeply felt commitment to his grandmother, Sarah.

In addition to helping students frame their discussions in a basic concept of story (such as the one provided by Leland Jacobs), and giving students language to use when talking about story, I also try to help students understand that each story is told and interpreted from a particular perspective. They need to recognize that the author provides one lens on the world, and their reading provides another. The more students know about the world, and the more perspectives they consider, the broader their interpretive lens will become. To accomplish this, I provide additional information about what is being read. For example, as we read stories that came out of World War II, I provided maps, which the students and I studied and compared, helping them to see that even mapmaking is a political act. I invited WW II veterans and Holocaust survivors to speak to the class from their experiences. I found and read letters written by soldiers from both sides of the war. I didn't always relate these events to a particular book, but time and time again students used them as a heuristic device as they struggled to make sense of the books they were reading and the characters they were meeting and trying to understand.

I intentionally select books to read aloud that are written by authors who I think portray, in accurate and authentic ways (Sims Bishop, 1993), the diverse peoples who represent multiple perspectives on the world. This deliberate effort helps students learn that an important goal in our classroom is not to homogenize the human experience, but to entertain multiple ways of understanding and being in the world. I also offer students articles by critics who disapprove of particular books because of their doubtful cultural accuracy and authenticity and ask students for their thoughts on the critic's perspective.

Literature Study Groups

About the first week in November, I usually invite five or six students to join me in a discussion of a particular book. We call these discussions Literature Study. All students are expected to join at least one literature study group each month for the rest of the school year. These studies provide a context for an intensive exploration of a particular book. Over a period of three or four days, we come together to think and talk about how and why particular characters in particular settings think, feel, and behave as they do. These studies offer me an important opportunity to see how well students are using talk to learn; how they are progressing in their abilities to listen to and consider views that differ from their own; or, conversely, how well they are hanging onto and defending views they believe to be true and fair and just. It is also a time when I can stretch students' imaginations, asking them to reconsider their initial reading from other vantage points.

I wait until November to begin literature study groups because, by then, many of the necessary elements for having a successful small-group discussion are in place: (1) students not in the study know how to work independently, so full attention can be given to the small group; (2) students in the group have had practice and feel comfortable talking to others about books; (3) students have begun to develop a particular way of thinking and talking about story; and (4) students have learned to listen and consider alternative interpretations.

Students need access to books that support deep reading—books that have characters who deal with life and its complexities in believable ways. Therefore, I set aside particular books from among which they can choose. Once the group has agreed on a book, students are given a week to read the book, and they are expected to come to the study group well prepared: They must have read the entire book and thought deeply about the characters they met, the relationships that formed among the characters, and the events that unfolded in the story. When we meet, we sit in a circle, either at a round table or on the floor, where we can speak and hear without strain or interruption. A circle symbolizes equal participation—all voices count. And, even though this may not be a reality, the circle constantly reminds me that issues of voice and access are at the heart of all we do; it is what we are striving for and what we consciously need to work toward.

My role in these groups is much like my role described above during read-aloud time. I validate and corroborate students' responses; and, when appropriate, I challenge students to reconsider their interpretations from new or different perspectives. I also take notes on what students say. This note-taking strategy serves two purposes: It moves me out of the discussion so that the responsibility for carrying on the conversation falls on the students, and it gives me an opportunity to find the topics that are significant to the particular group of students discussing the book. Usually I note responses that suggest a particular feeling about a character or event in the story. At the end of each session, I recap what has been discussed and ask students what they would like to explore for the following day. For example, while reading *Sounder* (Armstrong, 1969), one group kept using the word *prejudice*, but gave little evidence of what they meant by that word. The homework assignment that evening was to find and mark story events that show prejudiced behavior, which we discussed the next day. The discussion was, of course, embedded with the students' own experiences with prejudice. This led to a discussion about prejudiced behavior in different age groups, so that evening the students interviewed their parents or caregivers about acts of prejudice they had experienced, and those were the focus of the next day's discussion. The last day of the study, I talked to the class about some critiques of the book *Sounder* that had been made in an article written by Ann Trousdale. I asked the students to think about and discuss these arguments. (In Trousdale's article, "A Submission Theology for Black Americans: Religion and Social Action in Prize-Winning Children's Books about the Black Experience in America" [1990], she argues that the black characters in *Sounder* are presented as "docile, submissive towards whites, and accepting of injustice and oppression" [p. 1371].) The students had a hard time comprehending this perspective because they had been pulled along by the emotional impact of the story. However, when I compared it to stereotypes made about their culture (mostly Latino), they could understand why Trousdale's comments were important ones to consider. A few weeks later, I shared with the whole class a critique of *The Indian in the Cupboard* (1980) that accuses its author, Lynn Banks, of similar stereotyping of Indians. The students who had been in the literature study group on *Sounder* seemed more prepared to deal with this critique (whether or not they accepted it) than did the other students. This confirmed for me, once again, that the more practice and experience we have with particular strategies, the more competent we become in using them.

Literature study is contagious. Many students participate in literature discussion groups whether I am there or not. The sessions without me are less formal and are often sessions where students get together after reading a predetermined number of pages or chapters and talk their way through the book. Students often follow up these discussions with an art, music, or drama project that they later present to the whole class. These presentations are excellent ways of introducing books. Usually they result in lively discussions over who gets to read the book next. I sometimes ask students to tape-record these sessions. When I listen, I hear students validating, probing, and challenging each other. I hear them using the language of story to bring order to their reading experience: They attend to characters and their situations in the story world. I hear them telling their personal stories in an effort to clarify or make sense of a certain aspect of life. And I hear them comparing the book they are reading to other texts they have read or viewed (i.e. other books, movies, TV shows, etc.). These tapes are excellent tools to evaluate whether students are, in fact, buying into the goals set up for them.

Teachers who want to make effective use of literature in the elementary classroom, who truly want literature for all, face challenges that are both organizational and academic. We need to attend to both; otherwise, the likelihood of success is slim. However, when the challenges are successfully met, and the students tap into the various potentials literature has to offer, they learn and they grow. They discover that by reading widely and deeply, they not only have a wonderful way to spend time, they may even develop a better understanding of people whose cultures and experiences differ from their own. And in they end, they may come to a better understanding of themselves as well.

References

Armstrong, W. (1969). *Sounder*. New York: Harper.

Banks, L. (1980). *The Indian in the cupboard*. Garden City, New York: Doubleday.

Goodman, Y., Watson, D., & Burke, C. (1987). *The reading miscue inventory: Alternative procedures*. Katonah, NY: Owens.

Hamilton, V. (1974). *M. C. Higgins, the great*. New York: Macmillan.

Jacobs, L. (1980). On reading story. *Reading Instructional Journal, 23*, 100–103.

Peterson, R., & Eeds, M. (1990). *Grand conversations: Literature groups in action*. Richmond Hill, ON: Scholastic.

Sims Bishop, R. (1993). Multicultural literature for children: Making informed choices. In V. Harris (Ed.), *Teaching multicultural literature in grades K–8* (pp. 37–53). Norwood, MA: Christopher-Gordon.

Smith, K. (1993). *A descriptive analysis of the responses of six students and their teacher in literature study sessions*. Unpublished doctoral dissertation, Arizona State University, Tempe.

Smith, K. (1995). Children, literature, passion: Bringing it all together. In L. Rief & M. Barbieri (Eds.), *All that matters: What is it we value in school and beyond?* (pp. 193–200). Portsmouth, NH: Heinemann.

Taylor, M. (1975). *Roll of thunder, hear my cry*. New York: Dial.

Taylor, M. (1981). *Let the circle be unbroken*. New York: Dial.

Trousdale, A. (1990). A submission theology for black Americans: Religion and social action in prize-winning children's books about the black experience in America. *Research in the Teaching of English, 24*, 117–140.

Wojciechowska, M. (1964). *Shadow of a bull*. New York: Atheneum.

Lingering Questions

1. Often I find students who like to read books from only one genre (e.g., fantasy, science fiction, historical fiction, etc.). When I require them to select from a different genre, they sometimes resent it and go back to their preferred choice once they have met the requirement. Would students be better off making their own decisions about moving out of one genre and into another?

2. Some students who are not proficient readers need more attention than I can personally give them. What kind of support systems can I create to give them the support they need and deserve?

3. I sometimes do a lot of the talking during literature study sessions. I think my participation is useful because it demonstrates a particular way of talking about books, it makes the group focus on story events that might otherwise be ignored or slighted, and often it makes the students consider different ways of thinking about a situation. Are my justifications valid, or would the students do just as well without my input?

Resource Box 8

Classroom Connections by Karen Smith

The three forms that follow are used to organize, keep track of, and grade students in literature study groups. The "Literature Study Contract" is given to each student on the first day of the study, and we fill it out as a group. We record the title of the book and then decide together how many days we will need to complete the book. I usually encourage the group to read a book in five to seven days. They sometimes request more days if the book is especially long; thus the second row of boxes on the sheet. Once we decide the number of days, we divide the number of pages by the number of days and record the pages that need to be read each day in the appropriate box. I "check in" with students periodically throughout the week to make sure they are where they need to be. If they fall behind, we brainstorm solutions to get them back on track. For example, they may come in at lunchtime and read, or set their alarms a half-hour early, or read their book for literature study during silent reading time. When we come together for the first time to discuss the book, I talk to students to make sure they have finished the book. If they haven't, we make a plan, record it on the sheet, and then proceed with study. I usually call the parents of students who are not finished and ask their support to help their child complete his or her assignment.

The second form, "Literature Study (Daily)," is one I use to keep track of each day's session. I write in the names of the group members and then make five copies (one for each day of the week), which I keep in a folder labeled with the book's title. The comment section is where I take notes about what the students discuss. (I usually use the back of the form, too.) We negotiate the homework assignment each day; I record our decision on this form while the students record it in their homework folders.

On the last day of the study, students are each given a copy of the third form, "Literature Study (Final)"; they fill in their names, book title, and date. Then each student, in collaboration with me, fills in a grade for each of the categories on the top. We can refer to the second form if they are unsure of how they have done throughout the week. Once the top is filled out, I collect the forms. Then I go through the forms, a student at a time, and ask the group to talk about how each student helped him or her understand the story or helped contribute to new understandings. I take notes on the conversation. Later that day, I meet with each student to negotiate a final grade. Once we reach agreement, we both sign the form and the student takes it home for the parent to sign.

Name: _____
Date: _____
Book Number: _____

Literature Study Contract

I agree to read the book titled: _____

This book has a total of _____ pages. I will pace myself according to the schedule below.

I kept closely to my planned schedule: YES_____   NO_____

I finished the book on time: YES_____   NO_____

I did not finish the book. I am on page _____.

Below is my plan to finish the book:

Literature Study (Daily)

Group: _____   Date: _____

Names	Brought Book	Prepared for Discussion	Participated in Discussion	Comments

Assignment _____
_____
_____

Literature Study (Final)

Book: _____
Name: _____   Date: _____

	A	B	C	D	E
Brought Book to Study					
Prepared for Study					
Participated					
Completed Assignments					

Comments:

Overall Grade _____

Student's Signature: _____
Teacher's Signature: _____
Parent's Signature: _____

Reflection Point

Gloria Kauffman, a teacher from Arizona, takes a big piece of butcher paper and records what each student wishes to talk about regarding a book they have just read. Reflect on other strategies teachers can use to make sure that all voices are being heard in literature study. What strategies can teachers use to support real conversations rather than individual monologues?

Linking Authenticity and Advocacy in Assessment to Inclusion

Tomás Enguídanos

A special education teacher describes his work with colleagues and parents to build collaborative models for disrupting the language of failure associated with bilingual students. During one of the monthly parent classroom community meetings, for example, Enguídanos had his students teach their parents something they had learned. Some of the students held workshops for the parents including one on desktop publishing and another on poetry.

A uthenticity in assessment is clearly not just an issue in educational placement. For the teacher, it is the bottom line, informing us of our next instructional step for each student. When I received the psychological profiles on my 15 new students, I was struck by their similarities. Each report was virtually identical to the next, offering the same buzzwords and the same recommendations for each student! It was as if only the names and dates had been changed. In my experience, there is very little said in these psychological placement reports that informs my instructional practice in a way that helps my students.

The worst thing about these reports is their effect on a family's expectations of their child and on the self-esteem of the student. The initial psychological report and the monthly writing samples paint such a different picture of the student. But convincing parents and students, who for years have listened to the language of failure flowing from the school like a river, takes ongoing monthly meetings that focus on student work. It also takes building a different relationship between school and home. I want to share how this has taken place at my school, César Chávez School in San Francisco.

From *Primary Voices K–6*, 5(3), Aug. 1997, 47–50.

The type of discourse that we have in our monthly "high context" progress meetings is really quite a departure from the normally "toxic" assessment discourse in the public school setting. As I see it, there are three stages to the transformative process in which we participate:

1. *Teachers as advocates: Reflection on what has happened prior to the student's arrival in our class.*
   The initial stage is one of reflection upon the student's educational history, the family's participation in that educational process, and the often unspoken feelings about the apparent learning problems—mostly in literacy. Frequently, the discussion focuses on what the child is *not* able to do, even when the teacher team tries to shift the focus onto the child's strengths. In some ways, this reflection resembles mourning, and it may take more than one meeting to let everyone verbalize their concerns. During this process, small steps toward goals are overshadowed by how far the student still needs to go.
   Much of the language that parents use when talking about their child's apparent inability to learn to read and write reflects some level of clinical explanation; they use terms like "incapacitated," "sick in the head," "stupid," "lazy," and even "crazy" to describe their own child. This type of language reflects the pain of repeated failures in developing literacy, the feeling that their child knows "absolutely nothing," and the frustration of listening to school language that is incomprehensible and/or easily misinterpreted. Given the frustration and anger toward the school and teachers that family members sometimes express, it is understandable that they are often reluctant to meet, but they are usually pleasantly surprised at the difference in tone at our meetings as we focus on the student's progress.

2. *Collaboration between school and home: A more accurate picture of what the student is capable of; celebration of small steps.*
   The second stage is more gradual and involves forming a more realistic picture of what the student can do. It takes parents and students, and often teachers, some time to shift from low expectations to expectations that are appropriately high and within the student's zone of proximal development. The family appears visibly confused when they first see the student's approximations toward reading and writing; improvement has not been seen for a very long time. It is at this point that parents begin to see that the original assessments were not accurate—were, in fact, toxic. It is very moving to watch the face of a mother who thought her son would never read and write as she listens to him read a heartfelt journal entry about

the moment he realized he could, in fact, do that which everyone—
including himself—seemed to doubt he could do. The mother cried,
the son cried, hey, we all shed tears of joy. This is where true collaboration begins to take hold. At this stage, parents and students are
often very motivated, asking in advance to meet with the team.
There is sincere celebration of the tiny steps (and occasional leaps)
that the student takes each month. It is much like the natural celebration that takes place in early childhood development when all goes
well.

3. *Student and parents as advocates: High expectations, leadership in the
school and community.*

   The parents, the student, and the teacher, armed with an
authentic picture of what the child is capable of, are now ready to
look critically at issues of access and equity in the school community,
identify which strategies are effective for the student, and determine
what is needed as a next step. This means that we, as a team, can
look for entry points for inclusion in the regular bilingual class, and
can advocate for changes in the class that will facilitate success.
Parents often have mixed feelings about their children exiting from
the program because they want them to continue to progress. They
feel a strong sense of community. At this point, parents must be
encouraged to become advocates for what they know works for *their*
child. Students can do it, too. We have seen it happen.

   Recently, in a monthly parent classroom community meeting,
the students were asked to teach their parents something they had
learned in the first semester. They broke up into three groups. One
group taught poetry using shared reading and pocket chart reading
(this is complex, and has many steps!). Another group taught their
parents desktop publishing, including importing drawings and ZAP
pictures that the students had saved on the network. Meanwhile, the
third group taught the parents to make accordion books about
division, based on the book *The Doorbell Rang*. Parents made stories
based on food that the students love to eat. I roamed around video-
taping; I could feel everyone's confidence as they read to the parents,
wrote for the parents, coached the parents. They knew the strategies
that worked for them and could teach adults to use them.

   Often, a student who reflects regularly on what makes her or
him successful can provide leadership in the classroom where other
peers are emergent readers and writers. These students have the
confidence to take appropriate risks as learners. They can help other
children who are struggling. They can help teachers help these
students. Let me tell you about a student I'll call Marta, who came
into my class so confused over letter sounds that she literally froze in
terror during interactive journal time. We gave her a lot of support

with a combination of scaffolding during journal writing and shared reading, using an ABC wall chart created by the students. Marta was so Spanish-dominant that, although she followed most commands, we had never heard her speak a word of English. This made it all the more amusing and amazing when Leonardo arrived and took over her spot as the student who struggled most in writing—only he wrote in English! Marta took him under her wing and scaffolded with him during journals for weeks using the ABC wall chart in English! Finally, Leonardo was able to wean himself from this third-grade powerhouse of a teacher who, apparently, had quietly learned English without our realizing it. Students like Marta let us know when they are ready to exit the program.

Building Relationships

Last year, I began a collaboration model with Norman Mattox, who teaches a "regular" bilingual class. We actually split our classes in half; he taught math and science, and I taught language arts. We struggled with just the right system for moving the students back and forth, had the students work in cooperative groups, and reflected with each other on the needs of all of our students. We found that the special education students were able to participate fully in literature circles and writers' workshop with their peers from the regular bilingual classroom. They also participated in the school's math and science program. In fact, the students performed at the same level or higher than they did in the self-contained class. We felt that combining our strengths offered our best to all of the students.

This collaboration led other teachers to ask for some collaboration with what we call "the special day class." Perhaps it *is* really becoming a special education. Next semester we intend to expand the collaboration to include two regular bilingual classes and the special day class. The Optimal Learning Environment conditions and strategies (see Ruiz & Figueroa, 1995; Ruiz, García, & Figueroa, 1996) are leading the way.

Over the last year, our school has been experimenting with different models for supporting all of our emergent readers and writers. My role in the school has shifted from isolated special day class teacher to advocate for reading and writing schoolwide. The change has come slowly through several years of staff development with wonderful projects like OLE. We have had the support of an outstanding principal and a superintendent who believes in bilingual and multicultural education. We have had time to meet and work things out, struggle, and build a program that refuses to accept failure. We wrote grants to buy books and computers. Changing a school takes all this and more; we must have time for teachers to build relationships with one another.

This increased effort to collaborate with other professionals in the building and district has had a significant impact on my role. As Norman Mattox and I worked together, we were impressed by how much we had to offer; we each had strengths that enriched the teaching of the other. We each grew in that collaboration much faster than one normally does when teaching in isolation. I think it was our collaboration and the wonderful writing that his students did in my class that facilitated the shift in my role.

I am now consulted on a regular basis when someone has concerns about a student's progress. The conversation has shifted from a deficit model to reflection on the learning conditions and strategies that we now know help children become readers and writers, even those who get a late start. Through this dialogue, we reflect on our practice as teachers, including issues of status, language, and culture. The parent/teacher/student model of collaboration is now being used in other classrooms. When a child in our school is not learning, the last person we blame is the student.

References

Hutchins, P. (1989). *The doorbell rang*. Boston: Houghton.

Ruiz, N. T., & Figueroa, R. A. (1995). Learning handicapped classrooms with Latino students: The optimal learning environment (OLE) project. *Education in Urban Society, 27*(4), 463–483.

Ruiz, N. T., & Figueroa, R. A. (1996). *The OLE curriculum guide*. Sacramento: California Bureau of Publications.

Reflection Point

How might you go about creating a more culturally responsive classroom? What literacies do the students in your room have upon which you could build? What literacies do members of the community have (be it bricklaying, karate, jazz, gardening) that you might integrate and build from in your classroom?

Cultures of the Fourth-Grade Bilingual Classroom

Eileen Craviotto, Ana Inés Heras, and Javier Espíndola

The authors describe here how they use the cultural and linguistic knowledge of their students in constructing curriculum. One strategy they discuss is interviewing family members who they state become a cultural resource by sharing their knowledge, experience, and expertise with students. The data produced from the interviews were used in different ways such as creating classroom norms and expectations or creating immigration stories to help others understand the commonalities and differences among people.

Recently, Eileen's fourth-grade class took a field trip to listen to the local symphony play excerpts of various classical music pieces. While waiting in line along with about 400 other fourth- and fifth-grade students from the surrounding area, a student, Angel, came up to Eileen and told her he wanted to whisper something in her ear. As she bent down so that he could share this private thought with her, he said, "Teacher, there is a lot of white kids here." Eileen responded by asking how he felt about that, to which he replied, "I don't know, kind of funny."

Angel's observation merely expressed what we as a country are trying to understand—teachers, students, and families are faced daily with issues of language, culture, and socioeconomic differences. Often these issues are framed negatively. However, we feel that differences can be embraced and used in a positive way in the classroom.

The "we" refers to a teacher-researcher collaborative team composed of a bilingual teacher, undergraduates, and a university professor. In this article, we tell the story of how our collaboration influenced practice and how issues of culture, class, and ethnicity influenced our teaching and curriculum. At times, we refer to what

From *Primary Voices K–6, 7*(3), Jan. 1999, 25–36.

happened in the classroom as "our teaching" when all members of
the team were teachers as well as researchers working with the
students in Eileen Craviotto's classroom. At other times, we talk
about Eileen's actions to represent her actions as the teacher. At still
other times, we talk about the university students and what they
were doing and learning. This tale, then, is a collective one, so we
use Eileen's name in place of "I" or personal narrative since the
others present (Ana Heras and university students) were often part
of these events, either as helpers, interviewees, resources, or
documenters. Thus, in this article you will hear many voices and see
many people taking many roles. These roles were purposeful and
part of the potential of the culturally relevant curriculum that we
were collaboratively developing and exploring for both the fourth-
grade and the university students who lived in Eileen's classroom.

Introduction

Our collaboration began in 1992, when Ana was a Ph.D. student who
was introduced to Eileen Craviotto, a bilingual teacher, through a
teacher-researcher project of the Santa Barbara Classroom Discourse
Group. Our initial focus was on documenting the opportunities for
learning presented in the fourth-grade classroom. Gradually we
became more interested in the relationships between language and
culture (Heras, 1995). Our concerns centered on understanding how
classroom practices provide access to literacy (reading, writing,
speaking, and listening) in first and second language through the
students' home cultural resources (Ada, 1995).

As teachers, we worked to support the funds of knowledge or
home-based cultural resources (Moll, 1992), while ensuring students'
acquisition of the tools they need to succeed in school (Delpit, 1995).
Working as a team, we explored ways of moving away from traditional teaching to other forms of educating that respect students'
cultural values and that put questioning and discovery at the center
of learning (Ada, 1995; Nieto, 1992). We refer to this type of pedagogy as "culturally relevant," building on the work of Gloria
Ladson-Billings (1995; 1998), who argues that "it is not enough to
individually be an academic achiever and be culturally competent,
you also have to have a greater sense of community and be in a
position to critique your own education" (1995, p. 465) and to understand how social forces shape the experiences of others differently.
Three key pieces of her approach that we used as a framework for
our teaching were:

1. a focus on academic achievement;

2. a focus on the students' cultural competence, i.e., a focus on affirming students' identities as they are shaped by their communities of origin, while promoting awareness of other possible and available identities;

3. a focus on developing sociopolitical consciousness.

In putting these principles into practice, we found that employing a culturally relevant pedagogy is a long-term, praxis-oriented, and collaborative process. In our work together, praxis means "theoretically oriented action" (Giroux, 1988) that involves combining teaching and research. In this article, we present examples of the ways in which we created culturally relevant opportunities for learning for Eileen's bilingual students.

Who Were the Students in the Fourth-Grade Class?

The bilingual class was composed of 27 students, 23 of whom self-identified as Mexican/Chicano or Mexican American, 2 as African American, and 2 as White European American. There were 12 native Spanish speakers, 12 native English speakers, and 3 bilingual native speakers. As part of a university curricular experience, a partnership was established with the fourth-grade class. In this project, 20 undergraduates began visiting with the fourth-grade students to observe, understand, and support the younger students in their learning (see Resource Box 9). As part of this partnership, Ana Heras and Eileen Craviotto guided bilingual undergraduates in documenting the collaborative work. Thus, in this fourth-grade bilingual classroom, there were many different groups of students and many different teachers.

We have chosen the work of four fourth-grade students to provide a perspective on how a culturally relevant curriculum may work with students of different backgrounds. Almancio and Gerardo were Mexican American students who had been in the same city all of their lives and had attended McKinley Elementary School since kindergarten. They were academically strong and fluent in both Spanish and English. Alex, who was also born in Santa Barbara, grew up speaking only English and was a student with mixed background, predominantly European American. Oscar was a recent arrival from Mexico and had limited English proficiency at the start of the school year. We analyzed interviews conducted with these students, as well as their classroom work. We present those results in the following sections to illustrate our culturally responsive approach to teaching and learning.

Resource Box 9

> **Who We Are and How We Got Here:**
> **A Personal Study of Immigration to California**
>
> Fourth-Grade Students
> 1. Students conduct a tape-recorded interview using guiding questions brainstormed in the class.
> 2. Students transcribe and translate the recorded interview.
> 3. Students write about an interview of an adult on how they came to California.
> 4. Students analyze immigration waves during the century.
> 5. Students make their Immigration Books; text is supplemented with maps, photos, and art.
>
> University Chicano Studies Students
> 1. Students conduct interviews with community members, family members, and students in the local schools to understand more fully the educational challenges faced by the Chicano/a community.
> 2. Students volunteer in a local bilingual classroom helping students with academic work.
> 3. Students write about an interview conducted with a student in the local schools using historical landmark cases to illustrate the article.
> 4. The seminar is based on the concept of praxis (a mutual relationship of fieldwork and intellectual work) as a way to better understand the challenges the Chicano/a community has faced historically and continues to face.

How Did Students' Use of Their Cultural and Linguistic Knowledge Influence Learning?

Through our documentation of and dialogue about what occurred across the year, we identified six characteristics that made the curriculum and the classroom culturally relevant to the students:

1. families were actively sought as resources for knowledge generation;

2. multicultural literature was used as a resource for understanding perspectives;

3. students were regarded as active knowledge generators;

4. classroom dialogue was a fundamental aspect of classroom discourse;

5. the classroom was framed as an inviting space for exploration, learning, and dialogue among peers, students, and adults;

6. several languages were used in the classroom as resources for communicating and learning—the languages associated with the academic disciplines of social studies, mathematics, language arts, science, and arts education, as well as Spanish and English.

We will now illustrate the first three characteristics to show what this culturally relevant learning "looked like" and how it helped students use their home culture as a resource for learning in

Eileen's fourth-grade bilingual classroom. The description of each characteristic was created by drawing on discussions among the team, on student work, and on the field notes and reflections gathered by the undergraduate students. Thus, we show how the learning of the fourth-grade students, the teacher, and the university students was intertwined.

Families as Resources for Knowledge Generation

One way of learning about one's history and culture is to interview family members, who become a cultural resource by sharing their knowledge, expertise, or experiences with students. Using this strategy, Eileen had her students interview their families about immigration and respect. Students were given tape recorders as a way of documenting the interviews. The tapes were brought to the classroom, where the fourth-grade students transcribed them. Many times, these students translated the tapes when a parent spoke in Spanish and the student wanted to tell the story in two languages. The university students provided academic and linguistic support in their weekly visits to the classroom, helping with such things as translations and the meanings of certain words. With the information acquired from their families, the fourth-grade students created minibooks and wrote autobiographies. The value of this process, which provided an opportunity for these students to develop a greater sense of identity through self-reflection, was revealed when students shared their insights with their parents and others attending a family night event.

Eileen's students also explored the meaning of "respect" by interviewing family members and friends in the students' communities. In doing this activity, they had the opportunity to define the meaning of respect from their families' or friends' points of view, and then to compare these views to those of their peers. For example, across the definitions, five common concepts were identified: obedecer a los adultos (obey adults); respect elders, family, teacher, and neighbors; be nice to others; listen; and be kind to people. The fourth-grade students can see differences in the following examples from interviews. Oscar interviewed one of the research team members (Ana Inés Heras), who said that respect meant "escuchar a los demás con atención y colaborar" (listen to others with attention and collaborate with others). Gerardo's family said that respect was shown by "no tomar cosas jenas, no hacer burlas de las personas, y ayudar la gente" (by not taking things that do not belong to you, by not teasing others, and by helping people). Alex interviewed a friend of his dad who is of Russian origin. To this friend, by "giving Mom a hug and a kiss" you show respect for someone older.

Eileen and the students then used this knowledge to create norms and expectations for their own classroom behavior. The documentation by the university students showed that fourth graders became aware of the different interpretations for respect within the various cultures represented in their classroom as well as commonalities across cultural definitions. We believe that these rules (norms) were meaningful to the students because they were developed from family knowledge, thus enabling students to see the norms as something that was theirs.

As the year progressed students were given other opportunities to use cultural knowledge from home. They were asked to collect immigration stories from their families as a way to understand the commonalities and differences of people in California (one curriculum focus of fourth grade is California history). This active investigation of students' family histories was then related to the great waves of immigration to California in the early 1900s, as well as to current immigration waves (see Resource Box 9). Students learned about the processes and struggles involved in the immigrant experience through hearing their families talk and through writing Immigration Books. For the majority of the students, learning about the immigrant experience was related to immigration from Mexico (see Figure 9.1 for an example).

By conducting interviews and constructing Immigration Books, the fourth-grade students were able to gain perspective on their families' experiences or their own experience with immigration. For those who were not recent immigrants, the project served as a way to explore immigration through the experiences of family friends, prompting questions about their own history. For example, Alex did his Immigration Book about an uncle whom he said had recently moved to Santa Barbara from Rhode Island, broadening the concept of immigration to include movement within the United States. His uncle informed Alex of the conditions and climate in Rhode Island. He also gave Alex valuable information about their family. Alex carried his curiosity about his family's history to the fifth grade, returning the next year to visit the teacher to show her documents he had found pertaining to his family history.

In his Immigration Book, Gerardo mentioned that his father was born in Guadalajara, Mexico. He included a map of Mexico and located the state where his father was born. In the book he describes wonderful aspects of Mexico, such as the cities and people. Gerardo learned that his father came to the United States for a better life. In addition, he gathered important information about the process involved in coming to the United States. His father said, for example, "La mayoría del rato estaba espantoso" and "Duramos días, como tres o dos en el camino." (English translation: "The majority of the time it was scary. It lasted days, like three or two on the road.") Gerardo's book also included an illustration of the three-day

Figure 9.1.
Tina's Transcription of Her
Interview with Her Mother

Tina's Immigration Interview Transcription

T: por qué viniste a California?
M: porque aquí vivían mis papás y mis hermanos
T: cómo era de donde viniste
M: era muy bonito
T: cómo era tu tierra?
M: ahm, era a bonita pero a la vez, mucho calor.
T: qué te gustaba hacer?
M: me gustaba mucho jugar con mis amigos y salir a pasear
T: cuánto tardó el viaje
M: tardó tres días para llegar aquí
T: ¿qué hiciste cuando llegaste a California?
M: ahm, me puse a trabajar
T: ¿qué extrañas de allá?
M: ahm, mis amigos y a mis tíos
T: ¿qué piensas de que a los inmigrantes no los dejan pasar a California?
M: pues pienso que es algo triste
T: ¿por qué?
M: pues porque toda la gente viene a trabajar aquí para salir adelante para
       sacar adelante a sus hijos

struggle to the United States that his father experienced. The Immigration Book furnished Gerardo with thoughts about his father's native country, life experiences, and struggles. Thus Gerardo used the Immigration Book to collect information about his heritage.

We found that in interviewing family members about their experiences, challenging situations may arise for the students and their parents, since the topics of immigration and family history are sometimes difficult to address. For example, there were some family situations where students were not allowed to investigate their own backgrounds, or where their relationship with the family did not support this type of investigation. This was the case for Oscar, who refused to interview his family on this topic. When this occurred, Eileen provided an alternative. She suggested that he interview one of the "university regular visitors" to their classroom. Oscar chose to learn about Dr. Heras, who is originally from Argentina. Through his interview, Oscar acquired knowledge of Argentina's capital, cities, people, and physical appearance. He was also exposed to popular stories from Argentina. Even though this opportunity to interview someone who was not a direct family member was available to all students, only Oscar chose this option.

When the fourth-grade students were interviewed by the undergraduates documenting the process of writing Immigration Books, their statements showed us that they learned reasons people came to the United States, how and where these people came from, and the experiences they went through when immigrating; thus students met the goals of the California curriculum in a culturally relevant way. Students learned about such aspects of the interviewees' homelands as demographic information, culture, and traditions. For example, Almancio said he had "learned that a lot of people come over here to get a lot of jobs, money, and a better life." Oscar's statement, "me gusta y aprendo mucho de personas" (I like it and I get to learn a lot from people) illustrates that students liked the immigration project. Many indicated they would like to do more in the future.

These activities showed us how cultural resources of the family can be used for academic purposes in the classroom. They also show how we created a range of opportunities for students to learn about history in a meaningful way, as well as how this knowledge could be used to make the traditional curriculum live. Further, through interviewing, transcribing, writing, and discussing information, students gained opportunities to use language in different ways for different purposes. By putting inquiry in the center, students were able to learn ways of using cultural knowledge for academic purposes.

Multicultural Literature as a Resource for Understanding Different Perspectives

Although lived family texts were a central aspect of Eileen's language arts and social studies curriculum, literature from other authors was also important. We used literature about the students' cultural heritage as well as that of other cultural groups (see Figure 9.2). Eileen based her choice of literature on two premises: (1) the importance of providing students with books that are relevant to their experiences (Dernersesian, 1993) as well as to the experiences of other groups, and (2) the importance of presenting students with a framework to help them understand similarities and commonalities in experience. In this way, Eileen provided opportunities for students to use literary resources to understand their own cultural experiences and those of others.

The following examples show the types of relationships that students were able to establish. Many students established an explicit relationship between the book *My Name Is María Isabel* (Ada, 1994) and their life experiences and culture. In that book, a teacher mispronounces María Isabel's name, renaming her "Mary." The story is written to portray this young Latina's point of view. Irene and Gerardo commented during their interview with an undergraduate student that they saw themselves in the character because "we speak Spanish and we are both in the fourth grade" and because "our parents were from different countries."

Figure 9.2.
Multicultural Literature Used
in the Classroom

Multicultural Literature

Amelia's Road/El Camino de Amelia, by Linda Jacobs Altman and Enrique O. Sanchez. Lee & Low, 1993.

César Chávez, by Maria E. Cedeño. Millbrook, 1993.

Children Just Like Me, by Sue Copsey, with UNICEF. Dorling Kindersley, 1995.

Coming Home: From the Life of Langston Hughes, by Floyd Cooper. Philomel Books, 1994.

Cornerstones of Freedom: Malcolm X, by Jack Slater. Childrens Press, no date.

Great African Americans in Civil Rights, by Pat Rediger. Crabtree, 1996.

Hablemos del Racismo, by Angela Grunsell, translated by Teresa Mlawer. Lectorum, 1993.

Immigrant Kids, by Russell Freedman. Puffin Books, 1995.

It's Okay to Be Different/Está Bien Ser Diferente, by Ramona Winner. Brainstorm 3000, 1996.

La Carta de Derechos, by Warren Colman. Children's Press, 1989.

La Constitución, by Warren Colman. Children's Press, 1987.

Life Doesn't Frighten Me, poem by Maya Angelou, paintings by Jean-Michel Basquiat, edited by Sara Jane Boyers. Stewart, Tabori & Chang, no date.

Seven Candles for Kwanzaa, by Andrea Davis Pinkney. Dial, 1993.

Somos un Arco Iris/We Are a Rainbow, by Nancy María Grande Tabor. Charlesberg, 1995.

This Land Is My Land, by George Littlechild. Children's Book Press, 1993.

Un Libro Ilustrado sobre Martin Luther King, by David A. Adler, translated by Teresa Mlawer. Holiday House, 1992.

Who Belongs Here? An American Story, by Margy Burns Knight. Tilbury House, 1993.

Another interview between a university student and a fourth grader allowed us to see that the fourth-grade students were able to move beyond their own ethnic groups. The following example shows how this student made connections between Native Americans and an African American (Rosa Parks) while reading the book *This Land Is My Land* (Littlechild, 1993). The university student's field notes reported that "the student told me that it is important to her to call them Native Americans and not Indians because that's what they like to be called." She also made a connection to Rosa Parks by saying that "she didn't want to leave her seat and the Native Americans didn't want to leave their land." Although the student was not

Native American or African American, she was able to identify the similarity in challenges faced by both groups.

These examples show how Eileen helped her students address the questions that Angel's comment at the beginning of this article raised for us: How do we educate students to understand diversity and difference? The examples and student comments in this section show that when resources are provided (e.g., multicultural literature) and a framework is made explicit for exploring similarities and differences in experience, students can take up these opportunities to "make sense" of the experiences of humans, regardless of whether these experiences are directly related to their ethnic or cultural affiliations.

Students as Active Knowledge Generators

As part of the culturally relevant curriculum, Eileen provided students with an opportunity to choose a research project and present it to the rest of the class. This project allowed students to explore further and to discover other topics that were of interest to them. It gave them opportunities to see themselves as researchers and as constructors and producers of knowledge as well as learners (Dorta-Duque de Reyes, 1995).

Eileen introduced students to research by modeling inquiry procedures through a group study of Martin Luther King Jr. and César Chávez. She worked with the students to unveil the differences and similarities between the two leaders and the two cultures. While this was a group project, Eileen asked students to reflect on the information and to construct their own conclusions. She began the project by exposing students to information about César Chávez and Martin Luther King Jr. As part of this process, she asked students to compare the two men's lives using a Venn diagram. The next step involved students in acquiring further information to use in writing an essay. Eileen provided students with choices of where to go and how to gather information. Some students went to the library to acquire books; others used the Internet, and some asked the adults in the classroom (i.e., the teacher, teacher assistant, university professor, and undergraduates) for additional information. The undergraduate students visiting the classroom helped the fourth-grade students to reflect on the information and to put their thoughts in writing. In this way, the undergraduates shared their knowledge of how to conduct and report research with the younger students.

Through these assignments, students were further exposed to the history of African Americans and Mexican Americans. Once again, they had an opportunity to become familiar with the heritage, struggles, and victories of the two cultures. The essay by Gerardo revealed his understanding of how these leaders used a similar technique (the boycott) to fight for what they believed was fair. In this way, he was exposed to information about how a leader from his cultural group (Mexican) helped his people fight for their rights peacefully, as well as information about how members of the African American community exercised their right to fight peacefully. Gerardo wrote: "César Chávez fought for equality so people wouldn't be treated like slaves. He did this by organizing a boycott against grapes. Likewise, Martin Luther King Jr. fought for equality so that they would give blacks the same opportunities as whites. He did this by boycotting white businesses."

Essays like Gerardo's showed us that this research project provided students with further opportunities to reflect on the obstacles that Mexican Americans and African Americans experienced in history. The assignment also allowed students to realize that César Chávez and Martin Luther King Jr. overcame difficulties, fighting hard to do so. These men of color were portrayed as role models for the students. The students were then able to make links between these people and people in their own lives. As they were exploring this group activity, students were also exploring everyday people (and their struggles) through their research about families and friends.

The next step in the research process was to have students choose their own topics. For example, Oscar researched Benito Juárez. Gerardo gathered information on Pancho Villa, and Almancio searched for Jorge Campos. Oscar chose to audiotape his report and make a book on tape. This was an option Eileen provided for those who wanted to pursue it. In this way, she helped students use strategies from one context (i.e., the family interview) to support their work in a new context (i.e., making a book on tape). She also helped them build links to and expand on cultural knowledge they gained from one project and enabled them to use it in new ways in other projects. Cultural knowledge then was knowledge of how to do research as well as content knowledge.

Concluding Thoughts

The examples above portray some of the ways in which Eileen fostered a sense of inquiry in her students through using multiple texts. We described how students used a range of texts—some they wrote from family experiences, some created by taping interviews, some created through discussions, some shown to them in the form of movies, some read to them, some that were located in the library or their class, and some drawn as posters. Through these texts, students were able to use family knowledge as a resource and to connect it to other texts created in the classroom. They were also able to use English and Spanish as resources for reading, writing, listening, and speaking. In this way, their own languages were as valued as the languages of their families and others in their class and world.

We were able to see these connections because our collaboration rests on developing, documenting, and reflecting on our practices as well as those of the students (both fourth-grade and university). As our teacher-researcher team continues to investigate ways in which culturally relevant instructional models and practices are implemented in the classroom, our goal is to research this process and the knowledge that is produced to help others see the potential value of this curriculum approach. Using these ideas, we have come to understand that our classrooms (the elementary and university classrooms) are open spaces where all students are seen as critical learners whose ideas count. These ideas shape the curricular experience. By providing students with opportunities to become researchers or inquirers of their families, we helped them learn to read the world and the word (Freire, 1983, 1998), thus forging a link between home and classroom experience. We also found that this dynamic model of teaching and learning requires that our work as educators be in constant transformation, making teaching a learning process for all of us, and learning a process transformed by teaching.

References

Ada, A. F. (1994). *My Name Is María Isabel/Me Llamo María Isabel.* New York: Libros Colibrí, Atheneum.

Ada, A. F. (1995). Fostering the home-school connection. In J. Frederickson (Ed.), *Reclaiming our voices* (pp. 163–178). Ontario, CA: California Association for Bilingual Education.

Delpit, L. (1995). *Other people's children: Cultural conflict in the classroom.* New York: New Press.

Dernersesian, A. (1993). The role of Chicano literature in teaching Spanish to native speakers. In B. Merino, H. Trueba, & F. Samaniego (Eds.), *Language and culture in learning: Teaching Spanish to native speakers of Spanish* (pp. 26–44). Bristol, PA: Taylor & Francis.

Dorta-Duque de Reyes, S. (1995). Praxis: A journey within. In J. Frederickson (Ed.), *Reclaiming our voices* (pp. 180–196). Ontario, CA: California Association for Bilingual Education.

Freire, P. (1983). The importance of the act of reading. *Journal of Education, 165*(1), 5–11.

Freire, P. (1998). *Teachers as cultural workers.* Boulder, CO: Westview.

Giroux, H. (1988). *Teachers as intellectuals.* Grasby, MA: Bergin.

Heras, A. I. (1995). *Living bilingual, interacting in two languages: An ethnographic and sociolinguistic study of a fourth-grade bilingual classroom.* Unpublished doctoral dissertation, University of California, Santa Barbara.

Ladson-Billings, G. (1995). Toward a theory of culturally relevant pedagogy. *American Educational Research Journal, 32*(3), 465–491.

Ladson-Billings, G. (1998). A conversation with Gloria Ladson-Billings: An interview by A. Willis and K. Lewis. *Language Arts 75*(1), 61–70.

Littlechild, G. (1993). *This land is my land.* Emeryville, CA: Children's Book Press.

Moll, L. (1992). Literary research in community and classrooms: A sociocultural approach. In R. Beach, J. Green, M. Kamil, & T. Shanahan (Eds.), *Multidisciplinary perspectives on literacy research* (pp. 211–244). Urbana, IL: NCTE.

Nieto, S. (1992). *Affirming diversity: The sociopolitical context of multicultural education.* White Plains, NY: Longman.

Trueba, H. (1993). Culture and language: The ethnographic approach to the study of learning environments. In B. Merino, H. Trueba, & F. Samaniego (Eds.), *Language and culture in learning: Teaching Spanish to native speakers of Spanish* (pp. 26–44). Washington: Falmer.

Video References Used in the Fourth-Grade Classroom

America, America. (1963/1964). Writ., prod., and dir. by Elia Kazan. Warner Home Video. 169 min.

The Fight in the fields: César Chávez and the Farmworkers' struggle (PBS Special). (1996). Independent Television Service, dir. Ray Tellas and Rick Tejada-Flores. Paradigm.

The Kid. (1921). Prod., writ., and dir. by Charles Chaplin. First National. 52 min.

Malcolm X: El Hajj Malik El Shabazz. (1992). Xenon Video. 60 min.

Martin Luther King: An Amazing Grace. (1991). Xenon Video. 60 min.

Roots: The Next Generations. (1992). Prod. Stan Margulies. Warner Home Video, 686 min.

A Time for Justice: America's Civil Rights Movement. (1992). Guggenheim Productions. 38 min.

Lingering Questions

1. How does the teacher achieve a healthy balance between providing a strong skills curriculum and, at the same time, enabling connection with students' linguistic and native resources?
2. How does the teacher incorporate state and local objectives into a curriculum that uses students' familial and cultural backgrounds?

3. What are the characteristics of collaborative projects that give students the chance to create meaningful experiences for all participants?
4. How do you decide what to repeat and what to reshape in the next year? What is the most meaningful way to evaluate participation and achievement—grades, projects, papers?

Reflection Point

Now that you have read the articles in this section of the book reflect on ways that you have taken on the role of inquirer in your personal or teaching life. Then consider how you might create space in your classroom for students to explore everyday issues of personal relevance to them. Reflect on the following questions on an ongoing basis as a way of monitoring your attempts at developing an inquiry component in your classroom.

What new voices have I heard?

What new conversations have been started?

What structures have been put in place to ensure that these conversations continue?

Give the "Wonderful Questions Book" a try. A template is provided for you in the resource box in this section. Reflect on some ways that you could build or adapt an inquiry-focused curriculum using the questions your students jot down in their books.

Resource Box 10

Stapleless Wonderful Questions Book

Enlarge to fit an 8.5x11 sheet of paper.

This question is interesting to me because. . . .

My First Question

Wonderful Questions Book

A Stapleless book

by

This question is interesting to me because. . . .

My Second Question

Go online to
http://www.ReadWriteThink.org

read·write·think
International Reading Association   NCTE   marcopolo

Copyright 2002
IRA/NCTE
All rights reserved.

This question is interesting to me because. . . .

My Third Question

My Sixth Question

This question is interesting to me because. . . .

This question is interesting to me because. . . .

My Fifth Question

My Fourth Question

This question is interesting to me because. . . .

Created using ReadWriteThink's Student Materials, Stapleless Book interactive tool: www.readwritethink.org/materials/stapleless/index.html

continued

Use the following six steps to fold and cut your Stapleless Book. You will need scissors to complete this portion of the activity.

1. Fold your paper in half.

2. Fold your paper in half again.

3. Make one additional fold.

4. Open the sheet of paper to half and cut along the dotted line.

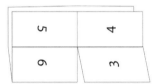

5. Open the paper and fold over to form a diamond, then push the sides.

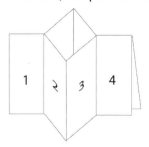

6. Push the sides and fold to form your book.

ReadWriteThink Web site:
www.readwritethink.org/materials/stapleless/index.html

IV Practices That Support Transformation

Practices that support transformation "involve the critical analysis and transformation of texts by acting on knowledge that texts are not ideologically natural or neutral—that they represent particular points of views while silencing others and influence people's ideas—and that their designs and discourses can be critiqued and redesigned in novel and hybrid ways" (Luke and Freebody, "Further Notes on the Four Resources Model," *Practically Primary, 1,* 99, 1999, www.readingonline.org/research/lukefreebody.html). More commonly known as critical literacy, these practices involve people using language to exercise power, to enhance everyday life in schools and communities, and to question practices of privilege and injustice by closely analyzing and reimagining or redesigning texts. "Texts" refers to such things as books, magazines, everyday print, and media texts such as television programs and television commercials as well as newspaper flyers and ads.

Comber ("Negotiating Critical Literacies," *School Talk,* 6[3], 2001, 1–2) states that this sounds grand but that often—perhaps usually—critical literacies are negotiated or developed by students and teachers together in the more mundane and ordinary aspects of daily life. "Critical literacies involve an ongoing analysis of textual practices: How do particular texts work? What effects do they have on the reader? Who has produced the text, under what circumstances, and for which readers? What is missing from this account? How could it be told differently? Critical literacy means practicing the use of language in powerful ways to get things done in the world. Questions such as these can be important catalysts in the process" (p. 1).

This section offers demonstrations of possibilities for constructing a critical literacy curriculum. We have included a brief introduction to critical literacy here knowing that the term itself may be unfamiliar to some readers. At the end of the book we have included a resource box of further materials on critical literacy practice.

Barbara Comber states that critical literacies involve an ongoing analysis of textual practices, that is, an analysis of what we read and write, why we read and write, and what purposes are served by our reading and writing, along with the impact that reading and writing have on individuals and communities. While participating in a critical literacy curriculum students and teachers together also use language to take up issues of power, privilege, and injustice.

Over the years, critical literacy has been defined in different ways. Allan Luke, in *The Social Construction of Literacy in the Primary School* (Melbourne: MacMillan,1994), talks about challenging texts—making visible selective versions of the world that are told to change conditions of living. Ira Shor, in *Empowering Education: Critical Teaching for Social Change* (Chicago: University of Chicago Press, 1992), talks about critical literacy as analytical thinking, reading, writing, speaking, or discussing. Patrick Shannon's *Text, Lies, and Videotape: Stories about Life, Literacy, and Learning* (Portsmouth, NH: Heinemann, 1995) argues that critical literacy content ought to stem from participants' lives and that the process should involve questions that develop from that content. Anne Simpson, in "Critical Questions: Whose Questions?" (*Reading Teacher, 50*[2], 1996, 118–127), talks about helping children to become conscious of how texts act upon them. As one could predict, varying definitions result in varying translations into practice. The "practice of critical literacy" described in the articles that follow are examples of some of the ways in which critical literacy has played out in classroom settings. As Comber notes, "[C]ritical literacy is not a finite set of practices" (2).

The articles by Vasquez and by Heffernan and Lewison show some of the ways that teachers help children learn to access, practice, and invent critical literacies. The teachers you will meet have made time for their students to begin to take an analytic perspective, to read the word and the world, to find out how things operate, to uncover what ways of being have maintained these ways of operating and what they can do to change the way things are. The last of the three articles, by Harste and Leland, provides an overview of how stories like that of Vasquez, and Heffernan and Lewison's work, enlarge the space of what is possible in a transformative critical literacy curriculum.

The articles included in this section are "Finding Our Way: Using the Everyday to Create a Critical Literacy Curriculum," by V. Vasquez, "Making Real-World Issues Our Business: Critical Literacy in a Third-Grade Classroom," by L. Heffernan and M. Lewison, and "Critical Literacy: Enlarging the Space of the Possible," by C. H. Leland and J. C. Harste.

Finding Our Way: Using the Everyday to Create a Critical Literacy Curriculum

Vivian Vasquez

The author shows some of the frustrations, pitfalls, and complexities she experienced while attempting to find ways of engaging with critical literacies in her kindergarten classroom. She considers what might happen if she were to use the everyday texts her students brought into the classroom to form the basis for doing critical literacy. Everyday texts include print artifacts from everyday life as well as stories from the community, along with texts from television and other media found in and around home as well as at school and other public spaces.

"I'm Jason, the Red Ranger."

"Okay, I'll be Billy the Blue Ranger."

"You be the Yellow Ranger."

"I can't be the Yellow Ranger. I'm a boy!"

In one area of the classroom a group of four boys were preparing themselves for a Power Ranger game they were inventing. In another area a group of children made drawings of their favorite Power Rangers.

Power Rangers were characters in a television show of the same name in which a group of teenagers transformed themselves into robotic superheroes. Once transformed these characters have special powers that allow them to keep Earth safe from alien invaders. Although my students were only four and five years old they were intrigued with the show.

As the school year progressed, I began to notice more and more activity and interest in Power Rangers, as evidenced by the children's dramatizations, conversations, and drawings. One of the boys shared what he had drawn. It was a blue shape that he said was triceratops, the Blue Ranger (see Figure 10.1). Noticing this, other

From *Primary Voices K–6, 9*(2), Oct. 2000, 8–13.

Figure 10.1.
Triceratops the Blue Ranger

Figure 10.2.
Power Ranger Drawings

children began presenting me with various Power Ranger drawings (see Figure 10.2).

A pair of children began chasing each other around the room in what they described was a Power Ranger episode. I could not believe how quickly these TV heroes had permeated our classroom curriculum. Unsure of what to do and feeling the tension of uncertainty with how to deal with the roughhousing that I believed would accompany superhero play, I heard myself saying, "All right, everyone. I think that it's about time that you took a break from all this Power Ranger activity. From now on, when you are at school I expect you to play, write, draw, and talk about anything but Power Rangers."

Later in the day, some time after this dictatorial comment was made, two of the children handed me some work they had done. "I made a bear," said one child. "I made a bear too," said the second child. Following close behind, a third child said, "Look, Miss Vasquez, that makes three bears" (see Figure 10.3).

In my journal I wrote:

> They made identical bears and there were another four or five children who had done the same thing. The children gave me what they thought I wanted. They were right. I wanted anything but Power Rangers so "anything but" was what they gave me. But making bears isn't the answer either. What is the answer? Where do I go from here?

As a preschool and elementary school teacher of 14 years, and one who attempted to frame her teaching from a critical literacy perspective, I know of the frustrations and pitfalls in attempting to construct a critical literacy curriculum. As the opening incident demonstrates, my frustration led me to censor all Power Ranger activity in the kindergarten classroom that I shared with 18 four- and five-year-olds.

In this article I share my frustrations and some of the complexities involved with constructing a critical literacy curriculum. I

Figure 10.3.
Matching Bears

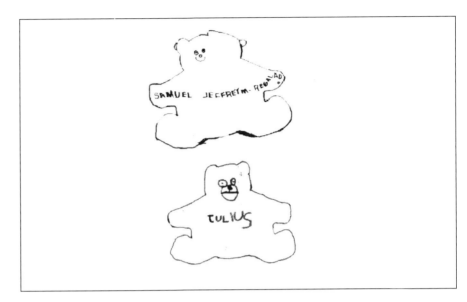

also explore what might have happened if I had taken up the issues that mattered in my students' lives (in this instance, Power Rangers) as text to form the basis for a critical literacy curriculum. Finally, I will share brief anecdotes of what happened when my students and I began to research ways of changing what could be said in our classroom about different groups of people.

Identifying Critical Incidents

The Power Ranger story is a critical incident, one that reflects an issue of social justice and equity, defined as an issue that results in the marginalization, disenfranchisement, disadvantage, or oppression of individuals, groups, or communities. Critical incidents create opportunities for analyzing the way things work that might lead to some form of social action. They may also be incidents that help my students and me to think about an issue in a different way.

Freebody and Luke's (1990) four essential literacies inform my reflections on the critical incidents shared here:

1. learning your role as code breaker
2. learning your role as text participant
3. learning your role as text use
4. learning your role as text analyst

According to Freebody and Luke, schools have been fairly successful at supporting children as code breakers (e.g., understanding alphabetic principles) and as text participants (e.g., using appropriate knowledge sources to make sense of text). However, I would agree with them in saying that we have not been as successful at supporting children as text users (e.g., knowing how to use particular texts in particular social contexts). Nor have we been very good at supporting children as text analysts (e.g., knowing how to ask questions such as, "How is this text positioning me?" "Who is this text written for?").

Revisiting the Power Ranger Incident

After reflecting on my dictatorial comment, and in an attempt to face my frustration in not knowing how to deal with the Power Ranger incidents, I decided to lift the ban. I hovered over my students, waiting patiently for an opportunity to talk about Power Rangers. I wanted the topic to be raised once more to give me a chance to construct curriculum differently. To counter my act of censorship I wanted to create a space where I could talk with my students about these TV characters and look critically with them at the content and implicit messages of the show. What I found, however, was that wanting to construct curriculum differently and actually making that happen were two different matters. It proved to be much more difficult than I thought it would be.

Not long after lifting the "ban," I noticed Kyle working on what I suspected was a drawing of a Power Ranger. "That's a Power Ranger," he shared. Kyle continued, "It's a pink one because my mommy likes pink (see Figure 10.4). I don't like the pink one, just the red one 'cause I like the color [red] better. Pink is a girl color, right? 'Cause men don't buy that color. 'Cause girls wear that color dress. My mommy sells clothes for kids so I know."

With this incident Kyle had opened the door to a conversation on gender. But despite my new resolve to create curriculum from my students' interests and the clear opportunity that Kyle's artwork and talk about that work presented, I was not able to deal with gender as an issue.

In retrospect I realize the incident with Kyle was not the first time that gender had been raised as an issue in my classroom. The four boys featured at the opening of this article were dealing with their own perceptions of gender when one of them said, "I can't be the Yellow Ranger. I'm a boy." At that time, however, I didn't even see the gender issue. I had neglected to look at how media construct what males and females can and cannot do, and at how much of an impact this was having on my students' perceptions of their roles in the world as boys and girls. I was too tied up in my own worries about superhero play and the potential roughhousing that might come from it to see the gender issue. I realize now that as I "hovered over my students waiting patiently for an opportunity to talk about Power Rangers," I was hovering with my own agenda. This became very clear to me in the incident that followed Kyle's explanations of why he didn't like the pink Power Ranger.

Figure 10.4.
Kyle's Pink Ranger

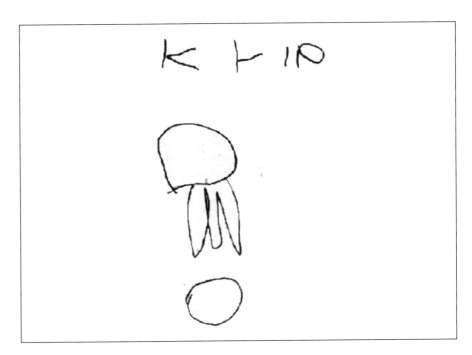

Sitting beside Kyle, Anthony spoke up, "I really like Power Rangers when they change to dinosaurs." In the television show, the Power Rangers are transformed into powerful animals that can fight viciously against evil forces. In response I said, "What would you think of Power Rangers if they turned into something else, like flowers?" He looked at me half-confused and half-amused, then walked away glancing back at me all the way.

In my response to Anthony, I was operating on my hope that it was not so much the fighting that was of interest to the children, but the *transformations* the characters go through from one thing into another. I was offering Anthony another possibility for what that transformation might be, and I imagine it was no accident that I offered him a symbol of something "peaceful" like a flower. My own agendas were clearly influencing the curriculum I was trying to create from my students' interest.

Later in the day, Anthony handed me a drawing he had done. It was a drawing of what looks like a person holding a flower (see Figure 10.5). Anthony had created what he said was a Power Ranger that had transformed into a flower. After quickly sharing his drawing with me, he turned away with paper in tow. As he walked away, out of the corner of my eye I could see him take the paper in both hands, crumple it into a ball, and throw it into the trashcan. At the time I was confused by the incident and angry with myself. I knew

Figure 10.5.
Power Ranger Transforming
into a Flower

that Anthony had made the drawing to appease me, but I didn't understand all the reasons why.

Power Ranger Literacy: Repositioning Super Heroes

This Power Ranger story helped me realize that I needed to listen to my students differently. I needed to position my own agenda differently by not letting it get in the way of my students' questions and the artifacts that they were creating and bringing into the classroom. If I really wanted to raise issues of social justice and equity as they emerge from my students, then I had to let that happen and be flexible with where that would take us. I knew that I would never be happy if I felt that students were simply engaging in social action to please their teacher.

"From a Bakhtinian point of view . . . part of children's developmental challenge is to learn to manipulate relationships, to achieve particular responses from others . . ." (Haas Dyson, 1997, p. 18). In what ways did Anthony manipulate our relationship in order to appease me into leaving him to engage in his Power Ranger play? The three students who created matching bears were acting under the same understanding and assessment of how this relationship worked. According to Haas Dyson, children appropriate cultural material to participate in and explore their worlds. What could I have done to offer them ways of framing their appropriations differently, in order to use this cultural material, such as the Power Ranger television show, as substance for reflection and social interrogation?

In retrospect, I now see how many opportunities I missed to create critical curriculum with my students. What if I had chosen to talk with Kyle and with the other children about the gender issues that were so clear in their Power Ranger play? So much powerful curriculum might have been generated. Each of the six rangers wears a particular color whether in uniform or not. Trini wears yellow and Kimberley wears pink. Pink and yellow are often thought of as "girl colors." The shades of pink and yellow used in the show are soft, almost pastel, in hue. The colors worn by the male rangers are darker and bolder: Zack wears black, Billy wears blue, Jason wears red, and Tommy wears green. One of the things we could have looked at is the use of color to position people in certain ways.

The colors represented not only gender, but specific cultural stereotypes as well. For example, in the original cast, Trini, the Yellow Ranger, ran the volleyball club. She was Asian. Zack, the Black Ranger, was African American. He ran the school's Hip-Hop Dance club. Tommy, the Green Ranger, and Jason, the Red Ranger, were both European American males. They were the leaders of the group. Beyond these stereotypes, Billy, the Blue Ranger, was the smartest in the group. He wore glasses. Glasses are often used to symbolize "nerdiness" or being a "geek." Kimberly, the Pink Ranger, was European American. She ran the gardening club and pined after the Green Ranger.

After the fact, I also recognized how popular culture, such as Power Rangers, is produced in the social use of commercialized items. I began to realize how Power Ranger paraphernalia determined who could take on what positions in our classroom. Having the latest in Power Ranger toys and clothing was a sure way into the Power Ranger clique that was developing. This clique quickly represented the dominant group in our classroom. Most of the members of the group were boys. How might we have interrogated this discourse to make visible the ways in which some children were being marginalized or disadvantaged because they didn't have the right Power Ranger "stuff"?

Not recognizing Power Ranger stories as literacy text prevented me from being able to use this text to get at some deeper underlying issues such as gender, power, control, racism, and cultural stereotyping. However, my reflections on the whole Power Rangers phenomenon in my classroom made me more aware of other critical incidents that would unfold in our classroom later in the year. This awareness helped me to focus our class curriculum around the sociocultural issues raised by my students through their talk, dramatizations, writing, and other means through which they represented their thinking. Once I began to frame our curriculum from the issues they raised, it became clear how we might engage in social action that would have an impact on my students' lives.

On one occasion, for example, the children wrote a letter to the chair of the School Barbecue Committee regarding the need to have vegetarian food at school events where food is being served. This action grew out of concern for a class member who could not eat at the school barbecue because he was vegetarian. The children's action resulted in the inclusion of vegetarian food on school event menus (Vasquez, 1999). On another occasion one of the girls wrote a letter to the Royal Canadian Mounted Police (RCMP) problematizing a publicity poster distributed by the RCMP. The poster depicted an all-male police force. Women were not represented. Along with Jessica's letter she included a revised version of the poster that included an equitable representation of males and females (Vasquez, 2000b). While reading the book *Baby Beluga,* by Raffi, a group of children problematized the discrepancy between the portrayal of belugas in the book and in a news item on television that spoke to the near extinction of beluga whales in the St. Lawrence River due to chemical pollution. To take up the cause of the belugas, the children engaged in fundraising and sent the money collected to the World Wildlife Fund of Canada (Vasquez, 2000a). In each of these cases my role was to engage the children in a conversation about ways to have our voices heard in our school and beyond. Then I had to support them with their writing as well as helping the children to identify helpful resources.

In a recent interview, Frank McCourt was asked how he identified the significant life moments that he wrote about in his Pulitzer Prize–winning novel *Angela's Ashes*. In response he said, "[N]othing is significant until you give it significance." His words resonate in my mind as I think about those things that I made significant in our kindergarten classroom. My experience with the Power Ranger incident certainly helped me to rethink not only what to make significant but the difference that what we take up in the classroom can make to help students understand the relationship between language and power.

References

Bakhtin, M. (1981). Discourse in the novel. In C. Emerson and M. Holquist (Eds.), *The dialogic imagination: Four essays* (pp. 259–422). Austin: University of Texas Press.

Comber, B. (1997). Critical literacies: Politicizing the language classroom. *Interpretations, 30*(1), 30–53.

Comber, B., and P. Cormack. (1997). Looking beyond skills and processes: Literacy as social and cultural practices in classrooms. *UKRA Reading, 31*(3), 22–29.

Edelsky, C. (Ed.). (1999). *Making justice our project*. Portsmouth, NH: Heinemann.

Freebody, P., and A. Luke. (1990). Literacies programs: Debates and demands in cultural context. *Prospect: Australian Journal of ESL, 5*(3), 7–16.

Haas Dyson, A. (1997). *Writing superheroes: Contemporary childhood, popular culture, and classroom literacy.* New York: Teachers College Press.

Henkin, R. (1998). *Who's invited to share?* Portsmouth, NH: Heinemann.

Lankshear, C. (1989). Reading and writing wrongs: Literacy and the underclass. *Language and Education, 3*(3), 154–174.

Lankshear, C. (1997). *Changing literacies.* Great Britain: St. Edmundsbury Press.

Maras, L., and W. Brummett. (1995). Time for change: Presidential elections in a grade 3–4 multi-age classroom. In P. Cordeiro (Ed.), *Endless possibilities* (pp. 89–104). Portsmouth, NH: Heinemann.

Morgan, W. (1997). *Critical literacy in the classroom.* London: Routledge.

O'Brien, J. (1998). Experts in Smurfland. In M. Knobel and A. Healy (Eds.). *Critical literacy in the primary classroom* (pp. 47–68). Newton, NSW: Primary English Teaching Association, 1998.

Vasquez, V. (1999). Negotiating critical literacies with young children. Unpublished dissertation, Indiana University.

Vasquez, V. (2000a). Getting beyond "I like the book": Putting a critical edge on kids' purposes for reading. *School Talk 5*(2), 3–4.

Vasquez, V. (2000b). Language stories and critical literacy lessons. *Talking Points 11*(2), 5–7.

Reflection Point

In Vivian Vasquez's classroom it is clear that underlying her attempts at doing critical literacy in her kindergarten classroom was the question of which literacies to privilege. Re-create the following chart and reflect on the article.

What literacies are dominant in Vasquez's classroom?	What literacies are marginalized? In what ways?
Which students would have access to Vasquez's curriculum?	Which students would not have access to Vasquez's curriculum?

Reflection Point

Think about your own classroom or a classroom you recently visited and reflect on what literacies you think were privileged in that setting. How do you know? What artifacts of learning and teaching provide evidence of this? Why do you think this happens? What ways of being and talking in schools maintains the privileging of some literacies and topics for literacy learning over others?

Making Real-World Issues Our Business: Critical Literacy in a Third-Grade Classroom

Lee Heffernan and Mitzi Lewison

The authors rethink the use of books in the literacy curriculum as a way to begin to create space for doing critical literacy in a third-grade classroom. Over the course of a school year, Lee attempted to implement a critical literacy curriculum in her classroom and Mitzi observed in the classroom as Lee's students negotiated this new terrain. The two met regularly to make sense of what was happening with individual students and the classroom curriculum, using field notes, student artifacts, and observations. The process caused them to interrogate their assumptions about children's interests, student learning, and what is appropriate curriculum in a third-grade classroom.

While listening to *The Bobbin Girl* (McCully, 1996), a picture book, Lee's third-grade students heard about how one of the Lowell girls, a mill worker, has to leave her loom because she is coughing. Later in the book, another worker is hit by a moving spindle and is removed from the factory. At this point, students interrupted the reading:

> *Mark:* This reminds me of *Lion to Guard Us* (Bulla, 1989), when the kids had to work all the time.
>
> *Beth:* And it's like *Ballot Box Battle* (McCully, 1998), when the girls couldn't learn the same things as the boys!
>
> *Jesse:* They don't even care that she's sick?
>
> *Lee:* Does it remind you at all of *From Slave Ship to Freedom Road* (Lester, 1998)? Remember when we talked about the fact that slavery was a business and the plantation owners wanted to make as much money as they could?

The kids talk among themselves. It's time to go to lunch and the children are very disappointed at not being able to finish the book.

From *Primary Voices K–6*, 9(2), Oct. 2000, 15–21.

While observing many such lively discussions in this third-grade classroom, we are struck by the insightful interpretations, the powerful connections to other books, and the thoughtful ideas these students share. Absent in this classroom is coaxing students to read and discuss books, basal-type comprehension checks, and the uninspired conversation that Villaume and Worden (1993) have observed in many literature discussions in whole language classrooms. What is happening in this classroom that has transformed third graders into serious interpreters of the books they're reading? How is it that they have become so interested in significant social and political issues?

In this article, we reflect on the events that occurred during a six-month period in this suburban classroom. We document the transformation that took place in learning and teaching as students took part in a critical literacy curriculum. Through this journey, we examine the significant curricular changes that can occur when the "real world" is allowed to enter classroom discussions and events.

First Steps— Interrogating Curriculum

At the beginning of the school year, the school librarian recommended reading the book *From Slave Ship to Freedom Road* (Lester, 1998). With its striking illustrations and wrenching text, the book seemed to be too upsetting for third graders. Lee kept the book for months, too uncomfortable with its content to read it aloud. Then she read Luke and Freebody's position that some kind of "fit" should exist between the delivery of literacy instruction and the "everyday beliefs and activities" of learners (1997, p. 198). After reading these words, Lee sadly suspected that there might be little connection, or crossover, between her whole language curriculum and the lives and beliefs of her students.

Luke and Freebody call for a new model of reading education, one that

> . . . shifts our classroom focus to the particular texts, discourses, and practices to which students have access and to the different kinds of social activities and cultural action that instruction can shape, encourage and yield . . . teaching and learning to read is about teaching and learning standpoints, cultural expectations, norms of social actions and consequences. (p. 208)

These words pushed Lee to reassess why the book *Slave Ship to Freedom Road* made her so uncomfortable. She began thinking about her reluctance to teach "standpoints." As teachers, we are frequently discouraged from using our position of power to persuade kids to adhere to certain beliefs. But as we struggle to keep our opinions to ourselves, we may be excluding important cultural issues from the curriculum. In the project we discuss here, students discussed a selection of books that show how people can begin to take action on important social issues.

From Slave Ship to Freedom Road: A Nervous Beginning

Students reacted to *From Slave Ship to Freedom Road* in a disturbing, but fairly typical way at first. A few kids smiled at the pictures of slave bodies in the sea and they giggled nervously when they heard that sharks would follow the boats and eat the slaves who were thrown over if they were sick. Others tried to put a positive spin on the topic:

> *Jesse:* If a slave was sick, he might make others sick, so it's better if he's thrown overboard.
>
> *Alec:* (looking at a picture of slaves waiting to be sold) They look like they're in pretty good shape to me.

In the past, we have noticed students taking similar cavalier stances when discussing characters with problems and those who live in poverty or are homeless. Students tend to make comments like, "Well, if they stayed in school, this wouldn't have happened." Perhaps this is not a desire to blame the victim so much as a desire for all problems to have quick and easy solutions. Would using these social issues books have an impact on these unsympathetic stances toward those in circumstances unlike our own?

In the lunch line that day, Jesse and Charlotte talked about *From Slave Ship to Freedom Road*. Charlotte said, "I had tears in my eyes when you read that book." Jesse added, "Yeah, get another book!" When asked if the book might be too upsetting for third graders Charlotte replied, "No, it's good to know about what happened."

The next day, the kids worked with partners and wrote responses to what surprised them about the book or what they wanted to remember. Sample responses include:

> "We were surprised that when the slaves were able to leave, they would not go because they had no place to go. Now that's surprising!"

> "It surprised us that they were chained up on the slave ships and couldn't move."

> "We want to remember that they threw the slaves overboard if the slaves were sick."

These written comments were very different from students' initial discussion about the book. They focused on what had upset them and their responses did not contain the denial statements that had surfaced the day before. Despite our initial discomfort with the book, *From Slave Ship to Freedom Road* had a big impact on the class.

Students referred back to this book many times during the semester. It became clear that students could discuss this powerful story without the roof caving in. Not only did they show no signs of being traumatized, but they displayed an amazing eagerness to talk about the book.

Whitewash: Beginning to Take a Critical Stance

The next book that students discussed was *Whitewash* (Shange, 1997), a picture book based on a series of true incidents. Helene-Angel, an African American preschooler, walks home from school with her brother, Mauricio, who isn't thrilled with this task. One day, a gang of white kids surrounds them, giving Mauricio a black eye and painting Helene-Angel's face white as they show her how to be a "true American" and "how to be white."

Books and other media on the topics of racism, gender, and class issues are often presented as "information" on a subject and are not used as beginning places for critical inquiry (Sumara & Davis, 1999, p. 199). With this in mind, *Whitewash* was chosen as a follow-up to *Slave Ship* to illustrate to students that racism is not a historical relic, something that was "fixed" long ago. This "it's no longer a problem" stance was evident in several students' responses to *From Slave Ship to Freedom Road*, where the ill-treatment of others was viewed as only an incident from the past.

The conversation around *Whitewash* made it clear that students had many questions about the books. They especially wanted to know why someone would do such a horrible thing to another person. Conversations focused on issues of citizenship. The kids made connections to an event in Bloomington, Indiana, which had happened several months earlier. Hate literature with racist and anti-Semitic comments had been distributed in many neighborhoods. An anti–hate-speech rally took place and many people in the town placed signs in their front yards that read "No Hate Speech." The class wrote a petition against hate speech and gathered the names from every student and adult in the building. They then posted their petition in the front hallway.

Because of this school-wide petition, issues of "hate speech" came up many times during the school year. Kids often adamantly pointed out, "That's hate speech!" if they heard insults or teasing. When they discussed *Whitewash,* the kids had many comments about the divisive power of language. Here is an excerpt from one such conversation:

> *Lee:* Many of you wrote this question on your response sheets, "Why did those people do that to her [Helene-Angel]? Do you have any ideas about that now?
>
> *Ann:* They called them mud people.

Sean: They said, "Do you speak English?"

Lee: Right. They also said that they were doing her a good deed—that now she could be American.

Hilary: That's hate speech.

Conrad: But she *is* American.

Blaine: She's African American.

Lee: Right. So are Americans only white?

All: A chorus of "no."

Lee: Well, so why do you think they did this to her?

Charles: They're mean.

Brent: They probably are stupid and don't know that people who aren't white are still American.

Although students are discussing serious topics here, they are not yet hitting issues of racism head-on in their conversations. At this point, they are beginning to realize that tough issues like racism and hate speech are legitimate topics for discussion in their third-grade classroom and that they have important things to say about them. As the semester progressed, students discussed many other books and some articles from the newspaper that focused on racism. The students were beginning to understand that racism and prejudice were alive and well in our world today.

Students wrote essays for the Bloomington Human Rights Commission annual essay contest. The essay topic was "Where Does Hate Come From?" The contest required that students examine how they could improve the atmosphere in their community. Rather than seeing hatred as "out there," they were to write about ways in which we all position ourselves against others. Kids wrote comments like, "We all have a little hate in us" and "I've spoken to people in a mean way before and I'm going to try not to do that any more." It was certainly atypical for children to be willing to risk making negative statements about themselves. Reading social issues books as a regular part of the curriculum laid the groundwork for this type of reflective thinking. It became "okay" to admit that prejudice was part of our culture, that it had affected all of us, and we all had probably participated in it.

Ian's Walk: From the Personal to the Political

Lee's classroom is directly across the hall from a special education classroom. An autistic boy named Evan ran into the classroom each morning for many months, touching the computers and playing with the water fountain until one of the teachers in the special education room would come for him. One day his teacher asked if he could sit in the beanbag chairs in the morning and look at books.

After several months of short daily visits by Evan, he gradually became a member of the class and stayed for longer periods of time. The students' interactions with Evan varied, but all seemed to enjoy having him there. Because of the kids' interest in Evan, *Ian's Walk* (Lears, 1998) was read and discussed. *Ian's Walk* is a book about an autistic boy and his sisters. This book explores not only the range of emotions Ian's sister Julie feels as a sibling to an autistic brother, but also the ways in which Ian himself experiences and senses the world "differently." On the journey to a park, Ian wants to smell bricks, not flowers, and once there, he lies with his cheek on the concrete instead of feeding the ducks. The book captures not only Julie's positive feelings toward Ian, but also her frustration and embarrassment.

The kids made many connections with Evan as they listened to *Ian's Walk*. Rather than relating to the sister, many of them related to Ian. The forward in the book makes it clear that a main purpose of the book is to explore the feelings of frustration that can come with having a disabled sibling. The kids had little to say about this issue. They instead wrote about Ian's feelings of frustration at not being allowed to do things his way. Michelle made a connection between Ian and Evan, "Evan loves to smell the chalkboard just like Ian liked to smell the bricks." When asked why she liked working with Evan so much, Michelle answered, "Because he is really fun to work with and a real fun guy."

A series of conversations and literacy events focusing on disabilities followed the reading of *Ian's Walk*. The kids had many questions about disabilities and had many of their own stories of their own disabilities ranging from bow legs when they were young, to hernias, to one classmate's blood disease. It became clear to the class that almost everyone had something that made them different—that people are never exactly the same.

This conversational strand continued as the kids discussed a narrative written by a young boy with leukemia, "Anthony's Story" (in Fleitas, 1999). A few of the kids laughed at a part of the story where Anthony recalls some of the questions he endured at school, "Why is your face so fat?" and "Why don't you have hair?" Their reactions were reminiscent of their first conversations about *From Slave Ship to Freedom Road*. After the reading, the kids made sketches of the ideas that stood out for them in "Anthony's Story." They seemed to rush through the sketches, seemingly having little to say about the themes in this piece.

The next day, when asked to share their sketches with classmates, the kids were able to sustain these conversations for a surprising length of time. Their sketches, though quickly drawn, did appear to contain many important ideas about how difficult it is for all of us to deal with illness and differences at school. When the class came back together, their conversation was animated and emotional:

Brad: Why did they ask Anthony those stupid questions?

Alec: Well, did they even know he had leukemia?

Drew: I don't think they knew it. That's why they asked about it.

Lee: Do you think the teacher should have talked to the kids about Anthony's disease or should she have given Anthony a chance to talk about it?

All: (in shouting tones) Yes!

Lee: Do you think it's a teacher's job to tell her students about this kind of information?

Jesse: Yes. The teacher just didn't get involved. Maybe she thought it wasn't any of her business.

Soon after this conversation, the students listened to an editorial from the local paper about a bill in the state legislature that would provide funding for services for people with developmental disabilities. The editorial quoted a spokesperson for The Arc, a national organization on mental retardation, saying that Indiana had "one of the poorest records of any state when it comes to serving people with mental retardation and related developmental disabilities." Indiana had been placed on a "Hall of Shame" list along with twelve other states. The kids were upset about this. "They don't have to put us down!" Jesse protested. Because of their connection with Evan, the kids felt very strongly about this issue. They wrote letters to their state senator.

Dear Senator,
I want you to please vote yes on this bill because we have a kid who comes to our class. His name is Evan and we want him to get services.
Kay

Dear Senator,
I support House Bill 1114. I want to get out of the Hall of Shame. We have a kid in our class. He is handicapped. I hope he gets the support he needs. Please help us.
R. J.

Dear Senator,
We support House bill 1114. We want to be on the Hall of Fame, not the Hall of Shame. Please, they need the money.
Eliot

In this set of conversations and events, we see these third graders making significant connections among books, personal narratives, news editorials, and their experiences with Evan. When they took the step of writing letters to their senator, the students were using literacy in a powerful way—one that not only communicated their feelings about a significant issue, but also used writing as a political tool to potentially make community changes.

In his description of critical literacy, Patrick Shannon writes about using literacy for liberation and activism, with an emphasis on making students' lives and the lives of others more just, equal, and free (1995, p. 88). Students in this classroom were certainly engaged in moving toward an emancipatory curriculum along with their teacher. Students and teacher together began to see how empowering it was to open up conversations about real-life issues in the classroom.

Reflections on Books and Beyond

Reading and discussing social issues books affected the classroom environment far beyond the regular reading time. Group meetings, for example, changed dramatically. Typically, prior to the project, students shared personal comments about their new glasses or weekend outings. After reading several social issues picture books, they began to share more stories from the news. At one meeting in particular, Brad reminded the class about our plan for organizing a bake sale for Posoltega, Nicaragua, Bloomington's sister city. Posoltega had been nearly wiped out by Hurricane Mitch and the local paper had many articles about the catastrophic conditions there. Erica told us about an oil spill that had happened in the Middle East. She had made a connection to an article the class had read about the animals that were killed by the Exxon Valdez spill. Angie shared about a man who was interviewed on the TV news the night before. She said, "He has Down Syndrome and he's an artist. They showed some of his art. He made a really great wolf. But he did say that some people make fun of him."

At another group meeting, the kids talked about a new proposed development in town that had been the subject of several articles in the local paper. They talked about how they hoped they wouldn't develop this site because deer grazed there and they liked watching them. Many decided to write letters to the newspaper expressing their hopes that the land would remain undeveloped. It was surprising to see the way group meetings frequently became places to discuss political and social, rather than personal, events. The literacy events in the classroom did appear to be filtering into "the everyday beliefs and activities" of students.

Perhaps the most important thing about bringing social issues books into the classroom is the enthusiasm the students have for these very different kinds of literacy events. Researcher Barbara

Comber noted that: "When given the opportunity for this kind of work, students demonstrated great energy and commitment, which left me as an observer with a great sense of optimism about the possibilities of working for social justice with students in school contexts" (1997, p. 26). The students in Lee's classroom were allowed to be caring, involved people who help others, who speak out, who have some power over the issues that confuse and trouble them. While teachers often fear that parents may object to students engaging in "controversial" issues, the parents of these children only made positive comments about the project. It was clear that many parents were actually discussing these topics at home with their kids, causing us to rethink assumptions about parental expectations.

We were able to learn so much from the children—to see what they could do when presented with challenging, real-world issues. Neither of us could have predicted their enthusiasm, their insightful connections between books and other texts, or their intellectual engagement in social and political issues. The books and the children's responses to them interrupted many of our long-held assumptions about what third graders are capable of achieving and what is an appropriate curriculum for young children. When Jesse criticized the teacher in "Anthony's Story" for not getting involved in Anthony's school problems, she said, "Maybe she thinks it's none of her business." We are convinced that enacting a critical literacy/social justice curriculum in elementary classrooms is definitely "our business."

References

Comber, B. (1997, April). *Pleasure, productivity and power: Contradictory discourses of literacy.* Paper presented at the Australian Literacy Educators and Australian Association of Teachers of English combined national conference, Darwin.

Harste, J. C., Breau, A., Leland, C., Lewison, M., Ociepka, A., & Vasquez, V. (2000). Supporting critical conversations. In K. M. Pierce (Ed.), *Adventuring with books* (4th ed.). Urbana, IL: NCTE.

Luke, A., & Freebody, P. (1997). Shaping the social practices of reading. In S. Muspratt, A. Luke, & P. Freebody (Eds.), *Constructing critical literacies* (pp. 185–225). Cresshill, NJ: Hampton.

Shannon, P. (1995). *Text, lies, and videotape.* Portsmouth, NH: Heinemann.

Sumara, D. & Davis, B. (1999). Interrupting heteronormativity: Toward a queer curriculum theory. *Curriculum Inquiry, 29*(2), 191–208.

Villaume, S. & Worden, T. (1993). Developing literate voices: The challenge of whole language. *Language Arts, 70*(6), 462–468.

Children's Book References

Browne, A. (1998). *Voices in the park*. New York: DK Publishing.

Bulla, C. R. (1989). *A lion to guard us*. Illus. Michele Chessare. New York: Harper.

Fleitas, J. (1999). Anthony's story, an RX for sore thumbs. *Teaching Tolerance*, Spring Issue, 52–55.

Lears, L. (1998). *Ian's walk: A story about autism*. Illus. Karen Ritz. Morton Grove, IL: Whitman.

Lester, J. (1998). *From slave ship to freedom road*. Illus. Rod Brown. New York: Dial.

McCully, E. (1996). *The bobbin girl*. New York: Dial.

McCully, E. (1998). *The ballot box battle*. New York: Knopf.

Shange, N. (1997). *Whitewash*. Illus. Michael Sporn. New York: Walker.

Reflection Point

Lee and Mitzi used books as a way to begin to explore possibilities for critical literacy. However, what is important to note is their realization that young children are very capable of and enthusiastic about taking up social and political issues. Taking up such issues as topics for study offers tremendous opportunity for children to engage in the analysis of text, how texts are constituted, and how they are constitutive. This kind of work, however, does not necessarily require the use of picture books. What are some other kinds of texts that could be used in a classroom to do critical literacy work? For example, how might you use popular-culture texts, magazine advertisements, or television commercials? How might the use of these other texts make this curriculum more accessible to different groups of learners? In the space below note other possible texts that could be used in a critical literacy curriculum.

Possible texts to use in a critical literacy curriculum	
1.	6.
2.	7.
3.	8.
4.	9.
5.	10.

12 Critical Literacy: Enlarging the Space of the Possible

Christine H. Leland and Jerome C. Harste

In this final article the authors note that stories like Vivian's and Lee's and Mitzi's are stories of hope and potential. They show how teachers can grow in their understanding of what it means to take a critical stance by attending to the tensions that come from children's questions as well as how critical literacy needs to be understood as a stance that is adopted consciously rather than merely as a unit of study.

There are several ways to think about the teacher's role in the teaching of reading. One important goal is to help children understand how texts work, including such elements as story structure and how sounds and symbols relate. Another goal in the teaching of reading is to help children understand that texts are open to a variety of readings given different histories, backgrounds, and experiences. Meaning making is central to the reading process. A third goal is to make sure that children experience firsthand how useful texts are in helping us see the world in a new light and accomplish work in a more efficient and effective manner. A goal that generally receives much less attention focuses on encouraging children to think critically about what they read—to pay attention to what a particular text is doing to them, how it is positioning them, and whose interests are being served by how the text is written.

A critical stance makes us aware that all texts are told from a particular point of view and are undeniably colored by this perspective. Whether we are reading a piece that is admittedly fictional or one that is said to be nonfiction, we need to be conscious of the assumptions that are embedded in the text.

A news story is a good example. Although it ostensibly presents factual material, an author's tone and choice of words can make a big difference. Our local newspaper, *The Indianapolis Star*,

From *Primary Voices K–6, 9*(2), Oct. 2000, 3–7.

often sets up an image of strife and failure when it refers to the Indianapolis Public Schools (IPS). Thus, a news story about improved test scores still manages to deliver a negative image with terms like "beleaguered IPS" and "embattled IPS." Reading from a critical perspective allows us to see this as a power issue. The owners of the newspaper have the power to hire writers who will "spin" stories to support their interests (e.g., vouchers and privatized education) and political positions. Since all texts represent particular cultural positions and discourses, being critically literate means being aware of how texts (and how we are taught to read them) construct us as particular kinds of literate beings. To be critically literate is to be able to decide for ourselves how we wish to be positioned in the world.

A curriculum built on critical literacy is one that highlights diversity and difference while calling attention to how we are constructed as literate beings. One theoretical model that offers a useful framework for thinking about critical literacy is Allan Luke and Peter Freebody's model of reading as social practice. According to this model, reading is best understood as a non-neutral form of cultural practice—one that positions readers in certain ways and obscures as much as it illuminates. Luke and Freebody argue that in preparing readers for the twenty-first century teachers need to help children develop their resources in several areas: (1) as code breakers, (2) as text participants, (3) as text users, and (4) as text critics (1997, p. 214).

Each resource area has its own set of issues. Approaching reading as a set of coding practices leads to an emphasis on analyzing the different sounds, marks, and conventions. Readers' efforts are focused on figuring out how texts work so that they can "crack" them. Seeing reading as a set of text-meaning practices leads to an emphasis on discovering how the ideas represented in a text string together and how cultural resources might help in the construction of different interpretations. An approach to reading built on pragmatic practices involves developing one's resources as a text user and leads to questions about options and alternatives for the here-and-now use of text, as well as predictions about how others will use it. Finally, paying attention to critical practices means that a reader becomes consciously aware of how texts position people and represent some voices while silencing others.

Working from Luke and Freebody's model, we want to make the parallel argument that teaching is another non-neutral form of cultural practice. As was the case with reading, different approaches to teaching represent cultural positions and ideologies as well. If we conceptualize teaching as a set of coding practices, the main goal is the transmission of knowledge and techniques. Inherent in this view is the belief that teachers simply tell or show students what to do. Prescriptive teaching manuals and "teacher-proof" materials are examples of resources that promise to help "crack the code" of teaching. The focus is on covering content without necessarily helping students to understand it. Approaching teaching as a set of meaning practices shifts the goal from rote learning to the development of individuals who are able to use cultural as well as text-based resources to generate a number of possible meanings. A view of teaching as pragmatic practices assigns top priority to the goal of developing an understanding of what can be accomplished in the real world. This view involves helping teachers see themselves as people who can change the school setting and create a different reality for their students. Finally, reimagining teaching as a set of critical practices means that teachers are able to help children critique and outgrow the systems in which they live and work. They become individuals who are motivated to interrogate their personal assumptions as well as those that are embedded in the educational and larger social systems in which they operate.

During the past two years, we have been investigating ways to support teachers in taking a more critical approach. Part of this work has focused on identifying children's books that are particularly useful for starting and sustaining critical conversations in classrooms. We have documented the conversations that follow the reading of these books to investigate how teachers and children become new literate beings as a result of having participated in these conversations. These books build awareness of how systems of meaning and power affect people and the lives they lead. The criteria we developed for selecting these books (Leland, Harste, Ociepka, Lewison, & Vasquez, 1999) include the following characteristics:

- They don't make difference invisible, but rather explore what differences *make a difference.*
- They enrich our understanding of history and life by giving voice to those who have traditionally been silenced or marginalized—we call them "the indignant ones."
- They make visible the social systems that attempt to maintain economic inequities.
- They show how people can begin to take action on important social issues.
- They explore dominant systems of meaning that operate in our society to position people and groups of people.
- They help us question why certain groups are positioned as "others."

Said differently, some books in the critical category focus more on historical issues like slavery or the Industrial Revolution and show

how large groups of people were marginalized and stripped of their human rights. Others are more contemporary in nature and encourage readers to interrogate current practices that are generally accepted as "what we have always done." For example, if a present-day high school uses the theme of "Slave Day" to raise money for student activities, is it okay because "it's traditional," or do we need to talk about how this practice might be seen as sustaining the degrading treatment of African Americans? Some books in this category focus on the issue of "otherness" and how our perceptions of "others" change after we get to know them better. "Others" can be people of different racial or social groups; they can be elderly or handicapped or sick; or they can be from another part of the country or the world. Engaging children in conversations about the pernicious effects of "otherness" can help them begin to see and understand the world in new ways. Like real life, many critical books do not have simplistic happy endings. The authors invite conversation by refraining from tying up their stories in neat little packages. Readers are expected to draw their own conclusions about what will happen next.

If we believe that democracy is a plan for human development that reflects a shared vision of "how things could be" (Fu & Stremmel, 1999, p. 5), then conversations like these are too important for children to miss. The notion of change is integral to this conception of democracy—there is no fixed standard, but an evolving set of fluid relationships among people over time. In some ways, this view of democracy is complex and messy. It doesn't lend itself to tidy categorization, and it's hard to manage. This view of democracy resonates with Davis and Sumara's (1999) suggestion that society as we know it is in the midst of a transformation regarding how we understand and describe the world. They argue that we are moving *away from* statistical analysis, causal logic, and a reductionist focus on linear relationships *toward* a realization that the universe is better described by complexity theory. According to this world view, complex systems (like living organisms) cannot be understood by examining their separate parts; the parts are as complex as the whole.

Davis and Sumara introduce the terms *simplexity* and *complicity*. They describe a simplex system as one that is dependent on initial conditions and suggest that in these systems, "the space of the possible is fixed" (1999, p. 23). By contrast, in complicity theory, interactions between and within the systems have the capacity to bring about "an opening of new possibilities, a continuous enlargement of the space of the possible" (p. 23). While they offer evolution and cognition as examples of complicit systems, we offer a critical approach to teaching as an example.

As teachers, we need to decide whether we want to maintain schooling as a simplex system or start reconceptualizing it as a complicit system where interactions among the participants have the capacity to bring about change and open up new spaces. Complicity also presumes that we are somehow implicated as an accessory, and no one is totally innocent of his or her actions. When teachers argue that they are "neutral" and don't want to bring up any ethical or moral issues in their classrooms, what they're really doing is supporting the status quo (Freire, 1971). "For us, complicity compels acknowledgement by those who dwell in the sacrosanct, unquestioned center that they too are thoroughly implicated in the unfolding of our cultural world—with all its inequities, injustices, and scabrous edges" (Davis & Sumara, 1999, p. 28). In other words, we all have our fingers in the cookie jar whether we want to admit it or not.

The realization of complicity relieves our feelings of guilt regarding the influence of our own values and agendas on our curricula. While we used to believe that our role as researchers was simply to observe and never to change anything, complicity reminds us that we "are inevitably engaged in transformation: each and every act, however benignly conceived, seeps beyond its intent as it enlarges the space of the possible. We are always already participating in culture making" (Davis & Sumara, 1999, p. 31).

When teachers share critical texts with children and talk with them about the issues raised by these books, they become deeply involved in the process of culture making. They "interrupt" (Davis & Sumara, 2000) current views regarding reading instruction and the topics of conversation that are appropriate for children (Leland, Harste, Ociepka, Lewison, & Vasquez, 1999). Teachers who reimagine teaching as a set of critical practices disrupt the normative patterns of society and open up spaces for new voices to be heard. Using selected children's literature is one way to begin critical conversations; they could also begin with newspaper articles, interviews with community members, or events in our schools.

Whitney Dotson, one of our recently graduated interns, is a new urban teacher who is actively seeking to enlarge the space of the possible. When her third graders were upset because the home of one student's grandmother had been condemned by the Board of Health and was scheduled for demolition, she urged them to take action by writing letters to the board. A sampling of these letters documents the new voices these children found while writing (see Figure 12.1). Instead of being positioned as helpless victims, they are positioning themselves as social activists who are challenging the status quo and asking for change. They are starting to understand the political capital that is inherent in language. Whitney is helping them (and herself) to understand that this capital is there for the

Figure 12.1.
Letters to the Board of
Health

> Oct 5, 1999
>
> Dear Bord of Health
> please please do not take
> peoples homes away from them
> if you do they will not have any
> where to go to. No where to sleep
> How would you like live on the
> streets and freete in the wintr
> that is how they are.
> Your friend
> Betty

> Oct. 5, 1999
> Dear Board of Health,
>
> Do not take peoples house away
> just because they dont keep
> it really nice licke you ant it.
> I dont licke it and when you do
> it to old people I really get mad.
>
> Codary!

> Octb 5, 1999
> Dear Board of Health,
>
> Please stop taking houses away from people
> I now that they are sad they are hungry and
> they want to eat and they need a
> please to sleep.
> They have no money to by a home. Where
> are they going to live at you give the people
> 4 chars to clean there homes you need to
> giv them a week or two to clean there home.

taking. We would argue that this is exactly what education should be doing—especially for the teachers and children of "beleaguered" public schools everywhere.

Reflection Point

According to Leland and Harste, using selected children's literature is one way to begin critical conversations; they could also begin with newspaper articles, interviews with community members, or events in our schools.

Think about topics or issues your students have raised in the classroom and pull together a set of books and other texts such as newspaper articles and magazine ads that support the exploration of those topics or issues.

References

Davis, B., & Sumara, D. (1999). Another queer theory: Reading complexity theory as a moral and ethical imperative. *Journal of Curriculum Theorizing, 15*(2), 19–38.

Davis, B., & Sumara, D. (2000). Curriculum forms: On the assumed shapes of knowing and knowledge. *Journal of Curriculum Studies, 32*(6), 821–845.

Freire, P. (1971). *Pedagogy of the oppressed.* New York: Seaview.

Fu, V., & Stremmel, A. (1999). *Affirming diversity through democratic conversations.* Upper Saddle River, NJ: Prentice.

Leland, C., & Harste, J. (1999). "Is this appropriate for children?": Books that bring realistic social issues into the classroom. *Practically Primary, 4*(3), 4–6.

Leland, C., Harste, J., Ociepka, A., Lewison, M., & Vasquez, V. (1999). Exploring critical literacy: You can hear a pin drop. *Language Arts, 77,* 70–77.

Luke, A., & Freebody, P. (1997). Shaping the social practices of reading. In S. Muspratt, A. Luke, & P. Freebody (Eds.), *Constructing critical literacies* (pp. 185–225). Cresskill, NJ: Hampton.

Reflection Point

The authors who have written from a classroom perspective in this section have all used their teaching to disrupt the usual classroom status quo. They provide compelling evidence that teachers with a critical perspective can change the patterns of interaction in classrooms and enlarge the space of the possible.

Since they are involved in complicitous research, they are not concerned primarily with describing or analyzing what is, but with finding out how what they are doing has affected the lives and situations of others. This kind of educational research is not simply research that takes place in educational settings; this kind of educational research is "research that seeks to educate and affect the way things are" (Davis & Sumara, 1999, pp. 31–32).

As a way to pull together your thoughts on this book, reflect on the ways in which the work that you do, your classroom practice, affects the lives and situations of your students. What difference does this make for your students in their lives at school? What difference does this make for your students outside of school? What difference does it make for your school community?

Concluding Thoughts: The Future Is Ours for the Making

The practices we as educators engage in make a difference, but only if we consider the kinds of literacies produced by those practices. We need to always ask questions such as, who benefits? In what ways? For what purposes? Do all my students have access to the curriculum? What difference will this curriculum make for my students now and in the future?

Education has to be more than rhetoric. In order to be effective, learners need to take on new identities and new agency. It is supporting this transformation of ourselves and our world that needs to be the focus of curricular work in the future. Education, like literacy, is never innocent. Even further, it is always about change, and, even more specifically, cultural change. While one can argue that education should preserve culture, in reality education has always been about changing culture. The trick, we suppose, is to continually revisit and rethink what we are doing. So, too, with literacy. Together teachers and students need to explore how practices such as making social statements and taking social action can become a social practice embedded in classrooms of the twenty-first century.

The practices we as educators engage in make a difference, and whether or not such practices make a "critical difference" depends on the social practices that surround their use. In the introduction we invited you to create a list of the social practices you already had going on in your classroom relative to access, meaning making, inquiry, and transformation. It is time to return to that list, to think about what new social practices you wish to engage in with the children in your classroom. The future, after all, is ours for the making.

Resource Box 10

Additional Resources on Critical Literacy

Boran, S., & Comber, B. (2001). *Critiquing whole language and classroom inquiry.* Urbana, IL: NCTE.

Christensen, L. M. (1999). Critical literacy: Teaching reading, writing, and outrage. In C. Edelsky (Ed.) *Making justice our project* (pp. 209–225). Urbana, IL: NCTE.

Comber, B. (2001). Critical inquiry or safe literacies: Who's allowed to ask which questions? In S. Boran & B. Comber (Eds.) *Critiquing whole language and classroom inquiry* (pp. 81–102). Urbana, IL: NCTE.

Comber, B., and Nixon, H. (1999). Literacy education as a site for social justice: What do our practices do? In C. Edelsky (Ed.) *Making justice our project* (pp. 316–351). Urbana, IL: NCTE.

Critical literacy (2002). *Language Arts, 79*(5).

Edelsky, C. (Ed.). (1999). *Making justice our project: Teachers working toward critical whole language practice.* Urbana, IL: NCTE.

Making curriculum critical (2000). *Primary Voices K–6, 9*(2).

O'Brien, J. (2001). "I knew that already": How children's books limit inquiry. In S. Boran & B. Comber (Eds.) *Critiquing whole language and classroom inquiry* (pp. 142–168). Urbana, IL: NCTE.

Vasquez, V. (1998). Building equitable communities: Taking social action in a kindergarten classroom. *Talking Points, 9*(2), 3–6.

Vasquez, V. (2000a). Getting beyond "I like the book": Putting a critical edge on kids' purposes for reading. *School Talk, 5*(2), 3–4.

Vasquez, V. (2000b). Language stories and critical literacy lessons. *Talking Points, 11*(2), 5–7.

Vasquez, V. (2000c). Our way: Using the everyday to create a critical literacy curriculum. *Primary Voices K–6, 9*(2), 8–14.

Vasquez, V. (2004). *Negotiating critical literacies with young children.* Mahwah, NJ: Erlbaum.

Vasquez, V. (Ed.). (2001) Critical literacy: What is it and what does it look like in elementary classrooms? *School Talk, (6)*3.

White, C. L. (2001). Examining poverty and literacy in our schools: Janice's story. In S. Boran & B. Comber (Eds.) *Critiquing whole language and classroom inquiry* (pp. 169–199). Urbana, IL: NCTE.

Primary Voices K–6: **Themes of Issues**

April 1993	Premier Issue	*Asking Questions/Making Meaning: Inquiry-Based Instruction*
August 1993	Volume 1, Issue 1	*Making Meaning through Writing: Writing to Learn*
November 1993	Volume 1, Issue 2	*Meaningful Change: Improving Teaching and Learning*
January 1994	Volume 2, Issue 1	*Challenge for Change: Theme Cycles*
April 1994	Volume 2, Issue 2	*Inquiry-Based Evaluation*
August 1994	Volume 2, Issue 3	*Generative Curriculum*
November 1994	Volume 2, Issue 4	*Conflict Resolution*
January 1995	Volume 3, Issue 1	*Talking and Learning in Classrooms*
April 1995	Volume 3, Issue 2	*Children's Literature for All*
August 1995	Volume 3, Issue 3	*Literacy Growth in a School Community*
November 1995	Volume 3, Issue 4	*Miscue Analysis for Classroom Teachers*
January 1996	Volume 4, Issue 1	*Re-Imagining Collaboration to Support Inquiry*
April 1996	Volume 4, Issue 2	*Establishing Patterns of Communities through Language*
August 1996	Volume 4, Issue 3	*Native Cultures in the Classroom*
November 1996	Volume 4, Issue 4	*Teaching Writers to Spell*
January 1997	Volume 5, Issue 1	*Assessment as Inquiry*
April 1997	Volume 5, Issue 2	*Classroom Curriculum and the Arts*
August 1997	Volume 5, Issue 3	*Learning in Inclusive Communities*
November 1997	Volume 5, Issue 4	*My Portfolio: Students and Teachers as Evaluators*
January 1998	Volume 6, Issue 1	*Making Connections: A School Family*
April 1998	Volume 6, Issue 2	*Literacy in Multiage Classrooms*
August 1998	Volume 7, Issue 1	*Talk that Empowers Struggling Readers*
October 1998	Volume 7, Issue 2	*Democracy in the Classroom*
January 1999	Volume 7, Issue 3	*Classrooms as Culture*
April 1999	Volume 7, Issue 4	*Teaching Young Writers the Elements of Craft*
August 1999	Volume 8, Issue 1	*Units of Study in the Writing Workshop*

October 1999	Volume 8, Issue 2	*Transforming Our Teaching and Learning*
January 2000	Volume 8, Issue 3	*A Research Community: Parent-Kid-Teacher Investigators*
April 2000	Volume 8, Issue 4	*Multicultural Language Practices*
August 2000	Volume 9, Issue 1	*Literature Circles: Growing Our Reading Lives*
October 2000	Volume 9, Issue 2	*Making Curriculum Critical*
January 2001	Volume 9, Issue 3	*Coping with Mandated Programs*
April 2001	Volume 9, Issue 4	*Literacy in the Arts*
August 2001	Volume 10, Issue 1	*Inquiry in Science*
October 2001	Volume 10, Issue 2	*Drawing on Experience*
January 2002	Volume 10, Issue 3	*Inquiry in the Classroom*
April 2002	Volume 10, Issue 4	*Reflective Learning Communities*
August 2002	Volume 11, Issue 1	*Telling Our Stories, Finding Our Voices*
October 2002	Volume 11, Issue 2	*Exploring Change: NCTE's Reading Initiative*

Editors

Vivian Vasquez is assistant professor in the School of Education at American University in Washington, D.C., where she teaches undergraduate and graduate literacy courses. Previously she taught preschool and primary school in Canada. Her research is focused on critical literacy, early literacy, inquiry, and social justice. Her latest publications include two books, *Negotiating Critical Literacies with Young Children*, published in 2004, and *Getting Beyond "I Like the Book": Creating Spaces for Critical Literacy in K–6 Settings*, published in 2003. Other publications include book chapters and articles published in *Language Arts, Phi Delta Kappan, UKRA Reading*, the *Journal of Adolescent and Adult Literacy, Reading Teacher,* and *Reading Today*. Vasquez has held appointive and elective offices in scholarly organizations including the National Council of Teachers of English, the American Educational Research Association, the International Reading Association, and the Whole Language Umbrella. More than anything she is proudest to be mom to T. J. Bilodeau, who has caused her to dream bigger than ever, and to be partner to Andy Bilodeau, who has been with her through the ebbs and flows of life.

Kathryn A. Egawa is currently serving as associate executive director at the National Council of Teachers of English, supporting the efforts of the elementary and middle-level membership of the Council and leading NCTE's national professional development project, the Reading Initiative. Egawa has spent more than twenty years in primary classrooms including three years as an elementary librarian. She and her colleagues continue their inquiries into alternative assessment, the practical applications of literacy theory, and professional development that builds from classroom contexts. Egawa has several publications including a coauthored book, *Beyond Reading and Writing: Inquiry Curriculum, and Multiple Ways of Knowing*.

Jerome C. Harste is professor in the Language Education Department of the School of Education at Indiana University, Bloomington. He has always been actively involved in professional organizations. As president of the National Council of Teachers of English (1999–2000) he advocated a diversity-and-difference model of education. Over the years he has chaired the Diversity Task Force within the National Council of Teachers of English, co-chaired NCTE's Joint Task Force with the International Reading Association on Critical Literacy, chaired NCTE's Commission on Reading and IRA's Sociolinguistic-Psycholinguistic Interest Group, and been on the Board of Directors of the International Reading Association. He also is past president of several literacy organizations. Harste is a children's book author (e.g., *It Didn't Frighten Me!, My Icky Picky Sister)* as well as author of numerous professional books and other publications (including *Beyond Reading and Writing: Inquiry, Curriculum, and Multiple Ways of Knowing; Language Stories and Literacy Lessons; Creating Classrooms for Authors and Inquirers; Whole Language: Inquiring Voices Want to Know;* and *New Policy Guidelines for Reading).* In addition, he has developed and hosted several videotape series, including *The Authoring Cycle* and *Visions of Literacy.*

Richard D. Thompson is currently an elementary teacher in Columbia Falls, Montana, where he has participated in such professional development efforts as the NCTE Reading Initiative and the Montana Writing Project. He has been a workshop leader and presenter at local and national venues, including providing district training as an NCTE Reading Initiative consultant. In the past he has presented at NCTE Annual Conventions and the Whole Language Umbrella. He has also served on the Elementary Section Steering Committee of NCTE. Thompson has several publications, including an article in *Primary Voices K–6* and a chapter in *Starting the Year with Whole Language.* In 2001 he received honors as Northwest Montana Teacher of the Year and the Montana Association for Teachers of English and Language Arts Distinguished Educator.

Contributors

In 1999 **Eileen Craviotto** was a fourth-grade bilingual teacher at McKinley Elementary School in Santa Barbara, California.

In 1997 **Tomás Enguídanos** was a special education teacher at César Chávez School in San Francisco.

In 1999 **Javier Espíndola**, a graduate of the Chicano Studies Department of the University of California, Santa Barbara, was pursuing a bilingual teaching credential at the University of California, Los Angeles.

In 1998 **Rosalie Forbes** was assistant professor and Reading Recovery Trainer at the Wheaton Campus of National-Louis University.

In 1998 **Sylvia Forsyth** was visiting assistant professor at the University of Iowa.

In 2000 **Lee Heffernan** was teaching third grade at Childs Elementary School in Bloomington, Indiana.

In 1999 **Ana Inés Heras** was a lecturer in the Chicano Studies Department and bilingual academic coordinator for Project ABRE at the University of California, Santa Barbara.

In 1997 **Carrie Kawamoto** was teaching kindergarten at the Kaala Elementary School in Wahiawa, Hawai'i.

In 2000 **Christine H. Leland** was associate professor of education at Indiana University–Purdue University at Indianapolis.

In 2000 **Mitzi Lewison** was assistant professor of education at Indiana University, Bloomington.

In 1999 **Isoke Titilayo Nia** was director of research and development for the Reading and Writing Project at Teachers College of Columbia University.

In 2001 **Elizabeth Olbrych** was teaching fourth grade at King's Highway School in Westport, Connecticut.

In 1998 **Susan Scheitler** was teaching second grade at Alexander Doniphan Elementary in Kansas City, Missouri.

In 1998 **Marcia Schwade** was teaching reading at Central City Middle School in Central City, Iowa.

In 1995 **Karen Smith** was associate executive director of the National Council of Teachers of English.

In 2002 **Amy Wackerly** was teaching grades 2–3 at the Center for Inquiry in Indianapolis, Indiana.

The late **Dianne Yoshizawa** was a first-grade teacher at Wahiawa Elementary School, Wahiawa, Hawai'i.

In 2002 **Beth Young** was teaching grades 2–3 at the Center for Inquiry in Indianapolis, Indiana.

This book was typeset in Avant Garde and Palatino by Electronic Imaging.
Typefaces used on the cover were Ellipse (ITC) and Agenda Light Ultra Condensed.
The book was printed on 60-lb. Accent Opaque Offset paper by Versa Press.